The Scholarly Communication Handbook

Every purchase of a Facet book helps to fund CILIP's advocacy, awareness and accreditation programmes for information professionals.

The Scholarly Communication Handbook
From Research Dissemination to Societal Impact

Lai Ma

© Lai Ma 2023

Published by Facet Publishing
c/o British Library, 96 Euston Road, London NW1 2DB
www.facetpublishing.co.uk

Facet Publishing is wholly owned by CILIP: the Library and Information Association.

The author has asserted her right under the Copyright, Designs and Patents Act 1988 to be identified as author of this work.

Except as otherwise permitted under the Copyright, Designs and Patents Act 1988 this publication may only be reproduced, stored or transmitted in any form or by any means, with the prior permission of the publisher, or, in the case of reprographic reproduction, in accordance with the terms of a licence issued by The Copyright Licensing Agency. Enquiries concerning reproduction outside those terms should be sent to Facet Publishing, c/o British Library, 96 Euston Road, London NW1 2DB.

Every effort has been made to contact the holders of copyright material reproduced in this text and thanks are due to them for permission to reproduce the material indicated. If there are any queries please contact the publisher.

British Library Cataloguing in Publication Data
A catalogue record for this book is available from the British Library.

ISBN 978-1-78330-624-4 (paperback)
ISBN 978-1-78330-625-1 (hardback)
ISBN 978-1-78330-626-8 (PDF)
ISBN 978-1-78330-627-5 (EPUB)

First published 2023

Typeset from author's files in 10.5/13 pt Revival 565 and Frutiger by Flagholme Publishing Services.
Printed and made in Great Britain by CPI Group (UK) Ltd, Croydon, CR0 4YY.

Contents

Figures and Tables	ix
About the Author	xi
Preface	xiii
Acknowledgements	xvii
List of Abbreviations	xix

1	**The Scholarly Communication Landscape**	**1**
	Introduction	1
	Key actors	2
	Where to publish?	6
	Research support and scholarly communication	7
	How to use this book	10
2	**Publication Types**	**11**
	Introduction	11
	Monographs	11
	Journal articles	14
	Conference proceedings	20
	Non-traditional publication channels	21
	Publication types and scholarly communication	25
3	**Open Access**	**27**
	Introduction	27
	The open access movement	27
	Green open access	28
	Diamond open access	30
	Gold open access	32
	Open monographs	33
	Open access at a crossroads	34
	Open access and scholarly communication	37
	Online resources	37

4	**Copyright and Licence to Publish**	**41**
	Introduction	41
	Copyright	41
	Licence to publish: exclusive and non-exclusive	43
	Creative Commons (CC) licences	45
	Rights retention strategy	47
	Copyright, licences and scholarly communication	48
	Online resources	48
5	**Peer Review**	**51**
	Introduction	51
	The peer-review process	52
	Traditional peer review	56
	Open peer review (OPR)	58
	Post-publication peer review (PPPR)	60
	Peer review and scholarly communication	60
6	**Research Metrics**	**63**
	Introduction	63
	Journal-level metrics	64
	Article-level metrics	67
	Composite metrics: h-index	69
	Data providers and coverage	70
	Matthew effect	72
	Responsible metrics	72
	Research metrics and scholarly communication	75
	Online resources	76
7	**Societal Impact**	**77**
	Introduction	77
	Planning for societal impact	78
	Ex ante and ex post impact assessment	83
	Social media: research and societal impacts	87
	Societal impact, social media and scholarly communication	90
8	**Research Integrity**	**91**
	Introduction	91
	Authorship	92
	Paper mills	96
	Reproducibility	97
	Retraction	99
	Generative AI: chatbots and more	100
	Research integrity and scholarly communication	101

9	**Critical Issues and the Future of Scholarly Communication**	**103**
	Introduction	103
	Oligopolistic publishers	104
	Open research	107
	Bibliodiversity, multilingualism and sustainability	109
	The future of scholarly communication	111
Case studies		**115**
	Case study 1 – Inter- or multi-disciplinary research	115
	Case study 2 – Preprints struggles	117
	Case study 3 – Scholarly appeal and public audience	118
References		**121**
Index		**131**

Figures and Tables

Figures

2.1	Publishing a monograph	15
2.2	Publishing a journal article	17
5.1	Peer review form: Example 1 (no specific questions)	52
5.2	Peer review form: Example 2 (with specific questions)	53
5.3	Peer review form: Example 3 (with specific questions)	53
7.1	The impact journey	77

Tables

7.1	Competence framework 'Science for Policy' for researchers	83
7.2	A framework for impact evaluation in grant applications	85
9.1	Price per article median value	104
9.2	Average price per article (APC) of OA journals by publisher size	105
CS.1	List of journals and their CiteScore and open access options	116

About the Author

Lai Ma is Assistant Professor at the School of Information and Communication Studies at University College Dublin, where she teaches in the Master of Library and Information Studies programme, including Scholarly Communication. Lai's research is concerned with research infrastructure, research evaluation and the political economy of information. She has published on the topics of information, research metrics, societal impacts and open access in the *Journal of Association for Information Science and Technology, Journal of Documentation, Research Evaluation, UKSG Insights, LIBER Quarterly* and others.

Preface

Scholarly communication can be a loaded term. It may sound like something that only belongs in an ivory tower. The misconception is understandable: academic publishers, peer review types and open access options seem irrelevant for most library work. But that is not true. In fact, scholarly works have significant influences on the education of future generations, as well as our cultural, social and political lives, public health and technological innovation. Scholarly communication is about understanding research and publication practices – essentially, it is about how knowledge is produced and disseminated. A basic understanding of scholarly communication is essential to comprehend and interpret journalistic pieces or social media postings involving terms such as 'peer-reviewed' or 'preprints' and to spot and stop potential misinformation and disinformation. In practice, scholarly communication is about supporting researchers in their publication process, dissemination and societal impact.

On reflection, my first scholarly communication conundrum happened when my very first article was accepted for publication. I was very lucky to be guided by my mentors throughout the publication process: selecting the appropriate journal, responding to peer-review comments and formatting the list of references in accordance with the house style. It was an exhilarating experience for a PhD candidate. However, when I was asked to sign the publishing agreement, I was not prepared to give away the copyright of the article – is this a common practice? Is there any way I can negotiate to retain the intellectual property of my work? But I was left with no option. Having a publication in a well-respected journal is essential for an early-career researcher. The publisher did not seem to allow any kind of negotiation, either. The automated system seemed to convey the message: transfer the copyright and get published or withdraw the article.

Not without reservations, the publishing agreement was signed and the copyright transferred. The excitement of receiving feedback (and perhaps recognition) from peers and the prospect of going on the job market with a track record overshadowed the vexed question of intellectual property. Then, some months later, I was asked if a translated version of the article could be published in a non-English-language journal. A meeting with a legal advisor was somewhat confusing: strictly speaking, I do not own the copyright of the article and hence cannot exercise any rights; then might there be leeway, since the translation would likely be different from the original article? Since then, I have learned more about the significance of a journal's reputation to the readership of an article; more importantly, I have witnessed and am witnessing the proliferation of online publications and alternative platforms, the normalisation of preprints, the rise of article-processing charges (APCs), the move to transformative agreements and the calls for research assessment reform. The need for understanding the many aspects of scholarly communication became apparent to me – not only as a researcher, but also as a lecturer in library and information studies.

My early exposure to the term 'scholarly communication' was associated with bibliometric and scientometric studies. Articles by Derek de Solla Price and Eugene Garfield were assigned readings and studies about the development and networks of science and knowledge fields were discussed. Today, some of these studies are referred to as 'science of science' or 'meta-science', while scholarly communication takes on a life in research support in academic libraries at a time of unprecedented and rapid changes. The status quo of traditional commercial scholarly publishers is being questioned, open access and open research infrastructure are emerging in every continent and copyright and licence to publish are under careful examination. All of these changes can overwhelm even the most experienced and prolific authors when complying with policy mandates and choosing the 'correct' open access option. Editors and editorial members are made aware of DORA, paper mills, ChatGPT, while finding it increasingly difficult to secure peer reviewers.

Due to the changing landscape, scholarly communication librarians and similar roles are in growing demand. First and foremost, they are to keep abreast of the latest developments of the scholarly publishing industry, policy mandates, new platforms for research dissemination. They run workshops and training sessions and provide individual consultation services. Many are involved in the management of research data and the negotiation of transformative agreements, while some are also active in professional association(s) and advocacy work. The key responsibility is to enhance researchers' research impact and networks, but sometimes scholarly communication librarians are tasked with the difficult job of explaining why diamond open access journals should be supported and why research metrics can be inappropriate and misused. Indeed, advocacy is much about education in the context of scholarly communication. For instance, many researchers may think that they know better, although they may have been misinformed about predatory journals or vanity publishers; and many are not aware that they have broken the law when they upload their publications online, not realising that they have given away the copyright or not understanding what copyright transfer entails.

The scholarly communication ecosystem is not isolated from society. Incomplete or inconclusive research can become sources of misinformation and disinformation, while reports of fabrication and fraudulent research can engender mistrust of researchers and research institutions. For one, predatory publishing and fraudulent research are symptoms of a hypercompetitive research culture. Until recently, these problems and issues have only been the concern of the scholarly communities, academic libraries, research institutions and funding agencies. However, scholarly works are increasingly available in the public due to the development of open access and the proliferation of preprint servers. It is a positive development insofar as incomplete and inclusive research findings are not interpreted as facts and misappropriated to peddle ideological ideas (e.g. Flat Earth).

'Change' is a keyword in the discourse of scholarly communication. Knowledge of and reflection on the many processes involved are necessary to understand what changes are urgently needed. In a presentation, the open access advocate Björn Brembs described the current scholarly communication system as a sinking ship, citing the affordability crisis and the reproducibility crisis. His warning may be perceived by some as immoderate, yet the matters are evident by the changing business model of both traditional and new publishers in recent times. For example:

- The editors of *NeuroImage* resigned en masse due to the publisher's refusal to decrease the article-processing charge (Imaging Neuroscience, 2023).
- An editor was dismissed by Wiley because he resisted the pressure to publish as many articles as possible to generate maximum author fees (Weinberg, 2023).
- Special issues and articles by publishers in the gold open access business (e.g. Frontiers, MDPI) have increased exponentially in the past few years.

It is also true that the vast majority of research studies cannot be replicated and their findings cannot be reproduced. Even if the system of scholarly communication is not in a pessimistic status of 'crisis', it certainly demands structural changes. The question is then whether these changes will be guided and negotiated by researchers and librarians, or will they be steered by government or commercial publishers? What are the roles and responsibilities of those who are involved in research support and scholarly communication?

The answers to these questions will be discussed and contested by the many actors in the scholarly communication landscape. This book is an attempt to provide the foundational knowledge for informed deliberations. Following the structure of a scholarly communication module, topics are discussed from different perspectives, guided by the question 'Where to publish?' The materials can be adapted by postgraduate programmes in library and information studies, as well as for career development training of PhD students. To a large extent, this book is written in a way that reflects on my experience: what would I have wanted to know as an early-career researcher? And what do my students need to know to make informed choices when they assist researchers?

I hope this book contributes to a fair, diverse and vibrant knowledge production future. Questioning where to publish is to shape the future of scholarly publishing and scholarly communication.

Lai Ma
Dublin, Ireland

Acknowledgements

I first taught scholarly communication in spring 2020. There was an obvious demand for the module: the scholarly communication landscape was undergoing rapid changes, to the extent that no one could claim to have kept up with all the open access options, transformative agreements, new policy mandates, research assessment criteria and alternative publishing platforms. This book is the product of four iterations of the module. My heartfelt thanks to my students for your patience and your engagement. I have learned so much from our discussions and debates and I would not have written this book without your encouragement.

My sincere gratitude to Liam Cleere, Michelle Dalton, John Cox, David Bennett and Aoife Quinn Hegarty, who shared their rich experiences and recommended useful resources and tools. Thanks also to Jane Buggle and Marie O'Neill, who led me to explore the world of library publishing. Michael Ladisch, now working in the other UCD (University of California, Davis), collaborated on my first project about bibliometrics and his knowledge and insights are most cherished.

The COST Action ENRESSH connected me to a network of researchers and practitioners who are enthusiastic and passionate about scholarly communication in its many aspects. My special thanks to Gunner Sivertsen, who hosted me at the Nordic Institute for Studies in Innovation, Research and Education and to Maria Biagetti and Aldis Gedutis for working together on the ethics of research evaluation at Sapienza University of Rome. Thanks also to Michael Oschner, Geoffrey Williams, Janne Pölönen and Ginevra Peruginelli for their kindness and support.

A scholarly communication handbook is essentially a collaborative work. All of the materials in this book, in one way or another, are 'stolen' from colleagues who have generously shared their resources and knowledge. I thank all of you.

I dedicate this book to my parents, who were not afforded the opportunity of formal education due to political unrest and migration. Their enthusiasm for education and learning brought me to the local library, where I spent most of my childhood. My father provided unwavering support even in the most difficult circumstances and has never questioned my ability and determination.

Finally, my thanks and love to my sons, Fields and Wolf. You are the best.

List of Abbreviations

AAM	Author accepted manuscript
ACS	American Chemical Society
AI	Artificial intelligence
APC	Article processing charge
API	Application programming interface
BPC	Book processing charge
BOAI	Budapest Open Access Initiative
CC	Creative Commons
CoARA	Coalition for Advancing Research Assessment
COPE	Committee on Publication Ethics
CRediT	Contributor Roles Taxonomy
DARIAH	Digital Research Infrastructure for the Arts and Humanities
DOAB	Directory of Open Access Books
DOAJ	Directory of Open Access Journals
DOI	Digital Object Identifier
DORA	San Francisco Declaration of Research Assessment
EOSC	European Open Science Cloud
ECRs	Early-career researchers
FWIC	Field-Weighted Citation Impact
HSS	Humanities and social sciences
IFLA	International Federation of Library Associations
ISI	Institute for Scientific Information
JIF	Journal impact factor
JRC	Joint Research Committee
LLMs	Large language models
LOCKSS	Lots of copies keep stuff safe
LPC	Library Publishing Coalition
NUP	New University Press
OA	Open access
OASPA	Open Access Scholarly Association
OJS	Open Journal Systems

OPR	Open peer review
ORE	Open Research Europe
PPPR	Post-publication peer review
PRFs	Performance-based research funding systems
REF	Research Excellence Framework (UK)
S2O	Subscribe to Open
SCI	Science Citation Index
SDGs	Sustainable development goals
SJR	SCImago Journal Rank
SNIP	Source normalised impact per paper
STEM	Science, technology, engineering and mathematics
THE	Times Higher Education
UNESCO	United Nations Educational, Scientific and Cultural Organization
URI	Uniform Resource Identifier
URL	Uniform Resource Locator
VoR	Version of record
WAME	World Association of Medical Editors
WoS	Web of Science

1
The Scholarly Communication Landscape

Introduction
Scholarly communication is a core competency in librarianship. It is essential for those who pursue a career in academic libraries, especially in the area of research support. It is also important for all who work in school, public and special libraries – because a basic understanding of the research and publication processes is necessary for assisting academic work at all levels. Indeed, it is of utmost importance that librarians can explain such terms as preprints, peer-reviewed publications and retraction in the context of information and media literacy.

Not long ago, physical copies of academic journals and monographs were housed in academic libraries, accessible only to those who are authorised to enter and read and perhaps make a few photocopies. There were no electronic databases or blogs or tweets, nor were there data products that analyse and compare research productivity and performance. There were no Creative Common (CC) licenses or open access models of different colours. Uploading a preprint was not an option and, in fact, researchers used to send their drafts to colleagues for comments by post! Today, researchers are faced with a multitude of publication channels, open access options and funding mandates.

In the last two decades there has been an increased demand for scholarly communication and research support roles in academic libraries. The development of online platforms and tools have led to unprecedented changes in publishing options, research assessments and research policies and consequently a transforming scholarly communication landscape. The tasks of a scholarly communication librarian can involve, but are not limited to, bibliometric analyses, publishers and publications advice, research data management and research dissemination and societal impact.

This chapter will provide an overview of the scholarly communication landscape by introducing the key actors and their complex and interrelated relationships, followed by a brief description of chapters with the key theme of this book: *Where to publish?*

Key actors

The primary role of scholarly communication librarians is to support researchers in publishing and disseminating research outputs in traditional and non-traditional venues. Answering the question 'Where to publish?', however, involves the understanding of the complex relationship of the key actors. In the following, the description of publishers, universities and research institutions, researchers and academic and research libraries aims to provide an overview of their contributions and interests in the scholarly communication landscape.

Publishers

Academic publishers play a vital role in the scholarly communication landscape, for the very reason that publications are the major medium in disseminating research findings and scholarly works. For many, the *Philosophical Transactions*, launched in 1665 by Henry Oldenburg and currently published by the Royal Society of London, is considered the first scientific journal (Csiszar, 2018; Fyfe et al., 2022), while the management of scholarly information can be traced back to the modern age (Blair, 2010). The number of academic publishers has increased significantly due to the expansion of research and higher education institutions in the post-war period. According to UNESCO, it is estimated that over US$2 trillion have been spent on research and development (R&D) annually in recent years, making academic publishing an essential component in research, impact and innovation.

The scale and business models of academic publishers can vary widely. Some publish both books and journals on a wide range of subjects, while some focus on specific genres and topics with a few titles. Some academic publishers are supported and subsidised by universities, libraries and learned societies, while others are commercially driven. Over the decades, there have also been scholar-led publications, many of them founded by those working in emerging and fringe research areas and methodologies before the traditional and mainstream journals and publishers would consider or accept them.

The sustainability of non-commercial publishers depends on institutional support. Most university presses are funded through or subsidised by the affiliated universities, although some operate as a non-profit entity (e.g. Cambridge University Press). Most library publishing programmes are maintained by utilising a small percentage of the library budget with the goal of fostering diamond open access (see Chapter 3). Traditionally, publications by learned societies and scholarly associations are supported by membership and subscription fees, while many now publish their society journals in collaboration with commercial publishers.

Currently, the majority of scholarly publications are published by commercial publishers. The so-called 'Big Deals' publishers – Elsevier, Springer Nature, Wiley, Taylor & Francis and American Chemistry Society (ACS) – each publish over 2,000 journals and together they occupy more than 50% of the market share of journal publishing (Fyfe et al., 2017; Stoy, Morais and Borrell-Damián, 2019). Together their subscription costs exceed 75% of total expenditures on journal publications. The global market of scholarly journals is expected to reach the value of US$28 billion in 2023 (Bhosale, 2022). In recent years, some commercial publishers have been expanding their business beyond publishing through vertical integration, providing products and services throughout the research lifecycle (Chen, Posada and Chan, 2019; Andrews, 2020). At the same time, there have been calls for public investment in open research infrastructure, for the predominance of commercial actors can become a significant barrier to reaching the goals of open access to scholarly information.

Universities and research institutions

In most parts of the world, universities are centres of higher education and research. Universities play a key role in providing research infrastructure and resources to support research activities, including library budgets for physical and digital resources, as well as the recruitment and training of professional librarians and paraprofessional staff in research support. At the same time, universities are also the employers of academic and research staff. The research assessment criteria for recruitment, tenure and promotion and internal funding schemes are aligned with a university's research strategy and priorities. Research planning can also be influenced by national priorities, as well as external funding schemes nationally and internationally.

Most universities are supported by public funds and are administered by governmental departments or ministerial bodies. In some countries, block grants for research in public universities are allocated through performance-based research funding systems (PRFs) such as the UK REF and the adaptation of the Norwegian model (Hicks, 2012; Cleere and Ma, 2018). These research assessment exercises are set to ensure the 'value for money' or 'return on investment' of public funding. Meanwhile, many universities participate in university rankings (e.g. US News, Times Higher Education (THE) and QS (Quacquarelli Symonds)). The ranking methodologies include research assessment based on a variety of factors, such as academic reputation, the number of citations and h-index (see Chapter 6). The criteria of research assessment set out by research assessments – both governmental and commercial – have a general effect on the so-called 'publish or perish' research culture.

Further, the requirements for public accountability and university rankings means that universities are expected to improve research performance and productivity over time and they have to monitor, track and assess research productivity and performance at university, departmental and individual levels. As a result, universities are consumers of benchmarking and reporting tools, as well as reports and consultation services for improving research performance. These tools and services are usually used by research management in strategic planning, but are sometimes also used to assist decision making regarding recruitment and redundancy.

Researchers

Researchers are the essential actors in the scholarly communication landscape: they are the authors, editors and peer reviewers of monographs, journal articles and conference papers, they are the leaders and members of learned societies and associations and some are involved in the management and organisation of scholar-led publications.

Researchers as authors: The nature of authorship of scholarly publications can vary in different disciplines: in the humanities and the social sciences, sole authorship (also called the 'lone author') and co-authorship of two or three authors are commonplace, whereas publications in the sciences (including health science) and engineering can have over tens of authors, often including those who are involved in a project though not necessarily writing the articles. The term 'hyperauthorship' has been used to describe co-authorships in the hundreds (Cronin, 2005; Nogrady, 2023). The Contributor Roles Taxonomy (CRediT) has been developed to designate the role(s) of a contributor, such that credits can be attributed in a fair and transparent manner. Researchers are encouraged and motivated to write and publish their work to advance knowledge. As authors, they are accountable and responsible for their work and their contributions are credited and recorded. At the same time, researchers are also under pressure to publish due to the use of metrics in research evaluation (see Chapter 6).

Researchers as editors: Scholarly journals and monograph series are usually edited by experienced researchers in a subject area. Series editors of monographs are a point of contact for potential authors: working closely with the managing editor of the publisher, they advise whether a manuscript may fit the scope and theme of a monograph series and they organise peer review of book proposals and manuscripts. Similarly, journal editors set the scope and objectives of a scholarly journal. They are responsible for screening submissions and selecting peer reviewers and issuing acceptance and rejection letters. Some publishers offer a honorarium for editors; however, editorial work is largely voluntary. As researchers progress in their career, editorial work is considered both as a privilege and a responsibility to shape knowledge production in their research area.

Researchers as peer reviewers: The majority of scholarly publications are peer-reviewed to ensure the quality of publications, involving the thoroughness of literature review, the validity and reliability of data collection and data analyses and the legitimacy of discussions and conclusions. Researchers are asked to peer-review manuscripts based on their subject knowledge and methodological backgrounds. Peer reviewers of monographs are sometimes compensated; however, the peer review of journal articles and conference papers is voluntary and uncompensated. Most researchers agree to be peer reviewers in the belief that their contributions are beneficial and essential for knowledge production and scholarly communication.

Learned societies and associations: In addition to research and teaching, researchers are often members and leaders of learned societies and associations, which maintain communities and networks of researchers outside their affiliated institutions by organising conferences, seminars and workshops. Some learned societies and associations also produce scholar-led publications, usually supported by member fees and subscriptions.

While researchers focus on their research and publications, they are not necessarily highly aware of the academic publishing market and the systemic changes in the scholarly communication landscape. The majority of researchers are acculturated to the so-called 'publish or perish' culture and the importance and significance of citations and citation-based metrics. As a result, researchers may not be paying attention to the good and bad practices of publishers, nor are they informed about the data tracking in research products and services. They may not know the differences between green, gold, or diamond open access models. They may even fall prey to predatory publications and conferences. The better they are informed, the better decisions they can make to share and disseminate research findings and to increase visibility and reputation.

Academic and research libraries

For decades, academic and research libraries have supported research and scholarship through collection development – that is, acquisition and provision of information, including books, journals and databases. The work of librarians has been somewhat invisible: when researchers are enjoying easy access to scholarly information, most are not aware that downloading an article in PDF involves the background work of careful budgetary planning, consultation with subject experts and negotiation of contracts. Libraries are also responsible for the maintenance of research infrastructure, including the library catalogues, institutional repositories and data archives, while librarians are engaged in the development of metadata and technical standards to ensure interoperability and sustainability of information systems.

The primary role of academic and research libraries is to support researchers and students by facilitating information access and by providing workshops and creating guidance documents, e.g. libguides. The provision of information is not an easy task, however, as it requires navigating the complex relationships between academic publishers, universities and researchers. Put another way, information access involves the negotiation with academic publishers, the research strategic planning of universities and the education and consultation services for researchers. At times, the interests of these actors can be in tension, for example, researchers working in an emerging area would request access to journals by non-mainstream publishers, but their demands may not be matched due to a library's budget constraints or a university's research priorities. Essentially, information access is a core value of librarianship, although the goal can be complicated by the market of academic publishing and other external factors such as funding mandates.

The evolving scholarly communication landscape means that academic and research libraries are faced with new demands, challenges and opportunities. In the context of scholarly communication, journals have moved from physical copies to digital formats and their subscriptions from individual to bundles, then the increased number of hybrid journals (journals with an option of article-processing charges) has led to the negotiation of transformative (or transitional) agreements. Research data management requirements, open access publishing mandates, science communication and societal impacts are all influencing the work of academic and research libraries, especially in the area of research support and scholarly communication.

Where to publish?

The chapters of this book are guided by the question 'Where to publish?' Publications are the most valued and important form of scholarly communication. Published research articles can inform researchers about the latest discoveries and findings and monographs are vehicles for in-depth scholarship and complex arguments. For early-career researchers, conference papers and posters are effective media for increasing visibility and soliciting feedback. Increasingly, researchers also opt to upload preprints and write for non-academic audiences. Meanwhile, the proliferation of both academic and non-academic publications, changing research assessment criteria and research policy, combined with the emergence of paper mills (see Chapter 8) and predatory journals (Chapter 2), have posed challenges for researchers to decide where to publish.

The answer to the question may seem obvious in the first place: researchers have been motivated and incentivised to publish in high-impact journals and with prestigious publishers. But why should researchers place trust in established publishers? And what are the considerations when researchers explore new publication venues and experiment with new forms of publishing? There are basic questions regarding different types of publications. What are the reasons for publishing a monograph rather than a journal article? Why should a researcher consider the frequency of publications? How to prepare a book proposal and negotiate a publishing contract? And then there are more questions when it comes to open access models, copyright and licensing, evaluative metrics and peer review. Each of these topics has been discussed widely in both scholarly and policy contexts, especially in the domains of bibliometrics, research on research (also referred to as meta-research), research evaluation and research policy. In this book, the discussion will be guided by the question 'Where to publish?' to include practical considerations for librarians and researchers to make decisions about academic publishing and research and societal impacts.

Further, researchers play an essential role in shaping the scholarly communication landscape by their choice of publication venues. They can initiate systemic shifts to scholar-led publications and mission-driven publishers by advocating for diamond open access publications and supporting emerging journals owned by publishers. However, most researchers are not up to date about the latest developments of the academic publishing industry and research policy. Scholarly communication librarians and related roles are vital because they can educate researchers through their work of research support. In explaining the differences between different open access options, they can elaborate on the implications for the future of academic publishing. Scholarly communication librarians can also elucidate the new trends in peer review which can shape the future of open research, while tackling issues pertaining to research ethics and research integrity. Further, the work of research support can reach beyond the traditional scholarly communication landscape as societal impact and research for policy (or evidence for policy) are becoming integral in research institutions, involving public engagement, science communication and, more generally, the use of social media and alternative publishing platforms.

Research support and scholarly communication

Scholarly communication is about communicating and sharing the hard work of research and scholarship with the goal of advancing our understanding of people, cultures, societies and nature. Until recently, the role of academic and research libraries has been collection development, i.e. purchasing and subscribing to the materials appropriate for and desired by researchers and students. The scholarly communication landscape, however, is undergoing rapid changes in the last few decades due to the switch to digital publishing, the drastic increase in the number of publications, the emergence of different open access models, the changes of research assessments and the call for societal impacts. The roles and responsibilities of research support and scholarly communication can range from bibliometrics and publishing agreements to the use of social media and research data management, depending on the needs of researchers in their institutions.

Publishing

Consultation services on publishing, including publication channels, book contracts and publishing agreements are central to research support and scholarly communication. Workshops, educational resources and individual consultation can be offered to explain the selection of publishers, journals and alternative publication channels, taking into consideration the target audience, potential research impact, as well as open access options and copyright and licensing issues. Support services can also be provided to guide researchers through the publishing process, including the preparation of book proposals and the negotiation of book contracts. Chapter 2 will discuss the publishing processes and considerations for different publication types.

There is an increasing demand for advice on publishing due to the changes in research policies (including funding mandates), business models and research culture. The choice of publication channels can be influenced by the criteria of research assessments, commitment to open access and disciplinary norms. Researchers do not necessarily understand the differences between the various open access options (i.e. green, gold and diamond) and their implications for the scholarly communication landscape. In Chapter 3, the pros and cons of the green, gold and diamond open access models will be discussed, with further considerations about copyright, publishing rights and licences covered in Chapter 4.

The peer-review process is often overlooked in the publishing process despite its being where decisions about acceptance or rejection are made. The types of peer review – double-blind, single-blind, open identities, open reports and so on – can be appropriate and beneficial for some, but biased and discriminatory for others. In Chapter 5, the peer-review process and types are considered from an author's perspective pertaining to the question, 'Where to publish?'

Bibliometrics

Bibliometrics are used in research assessments at individual and institutional levels, involving the use of indicators such as journal impact factor, CiteScores and field-weighted citation impact (Chapter 6). To assist grant applications and research planning, bibliometric tools (e.g. SciVal, Dimension) are often used to produce reports that trace and track funding sources and publication trends, compare citation impacts and benchmark research groups and institutions. These services require knowledge of a wide range of indicators and proficiencies in using bibliometric tools. In some institutions, bibliometric analyses are conducted to analyse collaboration networks and in-depth analyses, which require programming skills to work with APIs (application programming interfaces) and information systems.

As the responsible uses of metrics becomes an important topic of discussion amongst researchers, research managers and policymakers in recent years, librarians contribute to the conversation by offering workshops and seminars about the uses and limitations of bibliometric indicators, whilst some are involved in initiatives such as DORA (San Francisco Declaration of Research Assessment). The development of responsible metrics will be further discussed in Chapter 6. Relatedly, the overemphasis on research metrics has been seen as a cause for misconduct and manipulation in research, with increasing instances of retraction due to fraudulent research and other research integrity issues. Chapter 8 will discuss topics from ghost authorship and paper mills to generative AI.

Societal impact, social media

Researchers are increasingly encouraged to demonstrate the societal impact of research. Impact statements (or impact pathways) are often required in grant applications, for which researchers are to describe the potential impacts of their proposed research project. That is, how will a research project lead to tangible benefits and outcomes in professional or community practices? Or, how will a research project lead to technological innovations and job opportunities? Similarly, the impact case studies method has been used for researchers to demonstrate their achieved societal impact, ranging from influences on public and parliamentary debates to the eradication of diseases. As a result, societal impact is increasingly considered in research support, involving topics such as science communication and public engagement. Chapter 7 will discuss impact statements and impact case studies, with some tips for planning societal impact, including the use of social media and alternative platforms for widening dissemination of publications in scholarly networks and engaging in public discourse.

In the past few years there has been a strong increase in the use of Twitter, for example, as a scholarly public sphere where researchers share their work-in-progress, research outputs and resources, while some host and participate in journal clubs. Researchers make use of professional and personal blogs to engage a wider audience. Chapter 7 will also delve into researchers' considerations when using social media platforms and social forums, in relation to professional identity and time management.

Research data management
Research data management has become more important in the work of research support. Many funders require a detailed data management plan in grant applications, particularly in the context of open research. The topic is out of scope and is not covered in this book. Interested readers can consult *Exploring Research Data Management* by Andrew Cox and Eddy Verbaan (2018).

How to use this book
The structure of the book follows the journey of scholarly publishing to societal impacts. The concluding chapter discusses emerging critical issues and a call to action. It is not a book without acronyms or jargon, but readers can read from the beginning to the end, or simply jump into a chapter or a section of interest.

Where to publish is an important question for scholarly publishing and scholarly communication because different publication options serve different purposes and different interests; the more we understand them, the better we serve research and researchers.

2
Publication Types

Introduction
Monographs and journal articles are the major publication types for engaging in scholarly discourse and disseminating research findings, while non-traditional publication types such as blogs and podcasts have become more popular for science communication and public engagement. What are the differences between the publication types? What should an author consider when preparing a book manuscript and when planning to submit a journal article? This chapter provides an overview of the following publication types: monographs, journal articles and conference proceedings, as well as non-traditional publications including preprints and blogs, with a focus on the details which researchers should consider when selecting the right venue for publishing their work.

Monographs
There are different types of books: trade books, textbooks, 'crossover' (or research highlights) and academic books. Trade books are published for a general audience: they are distributed through booksellers and are available in general bookstores. Textbooks are written for educational purposes: they are mostly acquired by college and university libraries and are also sold in specialised and campus bookstores. Crossover books are academic research that has an appeal to a wider audience and written in a way that can be understood by non-specialists. They are distinct from traditional academic books in that they appeal to a wider audience, or to students, and are written in a more casual tone and style. In contrast, academic books, usually referred to as monographs, are long-form publications that represent original contributions and they are mainly aimed at researchers and scholars in cognate fields of study.

The following discussion mainly focuses on monographs, as they are the most important and valued form of scholarly communication, especially in the arts and humanities and humanistic social sciences. Monographs are usually between 40,000 and 80,000 words. If a manuscript is shorter than

40,000 words, an author should consider if it may be better published as journal articles or book chapters. Put another way, is a book-length manuscript necessary to fully develop an argument, a concept or a thesis? If a manuscript is longer than 80,000 words, an author may consider whether the scope of the project is achievable in a certain period of time. It is also important to understand that publishers have considerations other than the academic contributions: manuscripts of shorter and longer length can affect the costs of publishing, pricing and marketability. Monographs are usually purchased by university libraries and most books are first published as hardcover. Softcover copies are published when a book is expected to be purchased by individuals.

Book proposal

If a researcher intends to pursue a book project, it would be best to make initial contacts with a few publishers to discuss the topics of interest and potential audience. If a publisher is interested in your book project, they will invite you to submit a book proposal, including a synopsis of the book, a table of contents, a description of each chapter and a sample chapter. A full manuscript is not required at this stage. The synopsis of a book is for the potential readers to discern what the book is about, what is original and novel and why the book is worth reading. When a book has been published, the synopsis usually appears on the dust jacket or back cover, as well as promotional materials such as book catalogues and websites. Hence it should be written in a clear and accessible manner to appeal to the widest audience possible. The synopsis in a book proposal is no different, though the audience is limited to the editor and peer reviewers. The scope, themes and contents of the proposed manuscript are illustrated in the table of contents and the description of each chapter. These materials are tailored for the target audience and should demonstrate the breadth and depth of the contribution. The sample chapter is solid evidence that the book proposal has been well considered and not a preliminary idea, whilst it also provides some hints as to the writing style and tone.

Book proposals are usually peer-reviewed. Similar to the peer review of journal articles, reviewers will comment on the originality of your work and the significance of the contributions to the field of study. Peer reviewers will also be asked to suggest similar or competing titles on the market and the unique selling points of the proposed book. They also comment on the potential readers (e.g. students, researchers) and whether the book appeals to a wider audience. A book proposal also includes practical details: for example, what is the expected word-count of the book? When is the expected delivery of the completed manuscript? What are the potential channels for marketing the book? When a book proposal receives positive feedback from the peer reviewers, the publisher may offer advice on the scope and direction of a manuscript and then proceed with a book contract. The completed manuscript of an academic monograph will go through peer review before a book is accepted for publication. Upon acceptance, the book manuscript will go into the production stage: copyediting, indexing, typesetting, cover design and so on. The process usually takes at least three months. A proof of the book will be sent to an author for corrections and approval before going to 'print' – on paper or digitally.

Edited books and book chapters

Edited books include contributions by different authors. They can be major reference works, handbooks that cover the state of the art of a field of study, or a thematic collection. Some edited books are compilations of contributions to a conference or a symposium. The book proposal of edited books consists of the motivation and objectives, a brief description of the chapters, brief biographies of contributors, alongside practical details such as the word-count of each chapter, the total length and expected completion date. Edited books go through a similar peer-review process as monographs: in most cases, both the book proposal and the final manuscript are peer-reviewed before acceptance for publication.

Book chapters are contributions to edited books. Generally speaking, book chapters tend to allow for more provocative ideas and commentaries and 'think-pieces' which are not necessarily within the scope of journal publications. Contributors are encouraged to converse with other contributions in the edited volume. Book chapters are mostly valued in the arts and humanities and humanistic social sciences, but they are not considered as important as journal articles in STEM, on the basis that they do not present original and empirical research. Nevertheless, contributions to handbooks and similar tend to be read and cited widely.

Which publisher is right for you?

In *The Book Proposal Book* (2021), Portwood-Stacer suggests that an author should submit their book proposal to more than one publisher. One reason is that an author will learn more about the publishers through the book proposal process – their knowledge and experience in publishing works in the author's field of study, as well as the support and guidance a publisher offers. In addition, an author may also consider the following factors: open monograph, print and digital versions, distribution and marketing and copyright and publishing rights.

Open monographs are monographs that are freely accessible online. There are different formats: for some, the monograph is only available on a web page and the readers must read the contents online, meaning that the readers cannot bookmark or highlight the book. Most open monographs are also available in PDF and/or e-pub formats. They are free to download and readers can mark up the documents for their own use. Some open monographs are available in print and some are print-on-demand for readers who are interested in purchasing a physical copy. Open monographs may incur a book processing charge (BPC) to be paid by the author(s). These charges are usually supported by institutional or grant funding. Some open monographs are financed by publishing programmes such as subscribe to open (S2O) or library publishing (see Chapter 3).

A monograph or an edited book can be published in *print* or *digital* (e-book) format, or both. While many publishers currently publish in both formats, some only publish in print and some only digitally. For book chapters, a digital version may be assigned a DOI (digital object identifier) so that it can be located and tracked individually. The assignment of a DOI is particularly useful if altmetric (e.g. number of downloads, number of social media mentions) and citation-based metrics are deemed important in research assessments. An author would want to consult the publisher before signing a contract, especially if they have a strong preference for either print or digital format.

An author may also inquire about the distribution networks and marketing strategies of a publisher. This concerns whether a book will be distributed, that is, made available for purchase, view or download in different regions. Also, an author can also inquire whether a publisher promotes its titles in academic and professional conferences, on social media and via other channels. Understandably, an author is most concerned with the contents of the book; however, the publisher's distribution networks and marketing, as well as their publishing services in print and digital formats, can have significant impacts on the success of a book. Lastly, an author should consider copyright, publishing rights and licensing, which will be discussed in Chapter 4. Figure 2.1 opposite illustrates the monograph publishing process.

Journal articles

Journal articles are the major form of scholarly publishing in STEM (science, technology, engineering and mathematics) and some social sciences disciplines. Journal articles can include original research (or research articles), book reviews, short communications/commentaries and/or letters to editors. Research articles are considered most important in a research career, as they represent original contributions in advancing knowledge. Book reviews,

PUBLICATION TYPES 15

Publishing a monograph

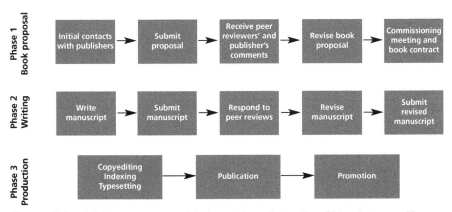

Figure 2.1 *Publishing a monograph* (adapted from University of Manchester, n.d.)

communications, commentaries and letters to editors are forms of scholarly communication where researchers can express their opinions about a journal article and more.

The scope of academic journals varies: some journals cover a specialised research area and others have a more general scope. In scholarly communication, a researcher should consider the intended audience: does an article address concerns or present findings that are of interest to peers who are specialised in the topic or methods? Or will it appeal to a wider audience in the field of study? Publishing in the right journal can improve impact by engaging with the right audience. So, what should a researcher consider when selecting a journal to publish their work? An essential step is to consider the aims and scope of a journal.

Which journal is right for you?

The aims and scope of a journal not only describe the research topics covered, but, if applicable, also the epistemological and methodological preferences. Some journals explicitly indicate that they only publish qualitative, or only quantitative, studies, some accept conceptual and perspectives pieces, while others may indicate strong preferences for specific topics and approaches. To get a sense of the aims and scope of a journal, a researcher can browse the recent issues of a journal: do the articles fit your interests? Would the authors of published articles be interested in your work? In addition, the editor(s) and members of the editorial board can speak to the journal's general areas and direction.

Oftentimes early-career researchers are encouraged to publish in the journals they read. It is because the aims and scope would likely be a good fit if the articles are relevant. Yet sometimes it is important to explore new journals to reach wider readership, especially when a research article is an interdisciplinary one that may appeal to more than one field of study. Readership is an important consideration when choosing a journal: established journals tend to have a sustained readership, while new journals can attract a niche readership in an emerging research area.

Once the aims, scope and readership of a journal have been established, a researcher should then consider factors that are time-sensitive: frequency of publication and the peer-review process. These factors are particularly important for early-career researchers if journal publications are required in the recruitment and tenure and promotion process. It can take longer for an article to be published if a journal only publishes two or three times a year. A prolonged peer-review process or a less frequent publication cycle can lengthen the time needed for an article to be published.

The frequency of publication can be easily found on a journal's web page, where the typical time period for peer review is also indicated. *Nature*, for example, indicates a rapid turnaround: (Nature, n.d.):

> Authors are usually informed within a week if the paper is not being considered. Most referees honour their prior agreement with *Nature* to deliver a report within seven days or other agreed time limit and send their reports online. Decisions by editors are routinely made very rapidly after receipt of reports . . .

However, the peer-review process of most journals usually takes at least 4–8 weeks. It should also be noted that peer review is an iterative process and an article may need several revisions. The journal *UKSG Insights* (UKSG Insights, n.d.) states that:

> The review period is expected to take around four to eight weeks, although this can vary depending on reviewer availability. Reviewers are asked to provide formative feedback, even if an article is not deemed suitable for publication in the journal.

The process and types of the peer review will be discussed in more detail in Chapter 5.

Next, the prestige and relevance of a journal is considered. The prestige of a journal is often associated with the journal impact factor (JIF) or CiteScore, because journals indexed on Scopus or Web of Science Core Collection indexes are commonly recognised as of good repute. There are also rankings of journals such as the Scimago Journal & Country Rank (www.scimagojr.com). Journals listed on these indexes and rankings are generally recognised in research assessments. It should be noted, however, that the coverage of these indexes is stronger in STEM disciplines and can miss important publications in the humanities and social sciences (HSS). Hence, HSS researchers use other criteria in determining the prestige and quality of a journal; for example by looking at members of an editorial board and by seeking advice from senior researchers and scholars in the field of study. Researchers should also note that indicators can sometimes be misleading, especially when comparing established with emerging journals, or general with specialised journals (see Chapter 6).

Finally, publishing open access is increasingly important. Fully open access journals are indexed on the Directory of Open Access Journals (DOAJ) representing both gold and diamond (or 'platinum') open access journals, while hybrid journals are subscription-based journals with the option for open access if the author(s) pay an article-processing charge (APC). The two main considerations are: first, if a research project is under a funding mandate to publish open access; and second, if the APC is supported by grants, transformative agreements, or other means. The green, gold and diamond open access models and related topics are discussed in Chapter 3.

Figure 2.2 sums up the criteria to be considered for publishing a journal article.

Figure 2.2 *Publishing a journal article*

Journal policies and author guidelines

Before submission, it is necessary to review the journal (or editorial) policies and author guidelines. Journal policies provide information about the aims and scope, frequency of publication, peer review and open access options that are the key considerations for selecting a journal, while some also include policies regarding authorship, reproducibility, competing interests, corrections and retractions, as well as misconduct and complaints.

As it has become common for authors to upload preprints before an article has been accepted, it is vital to review the preprint policy before doing so. Although many publishers allow preprints to be deposited before submission, some indicate specific conditions. The *UKSG Insights* (UKSG Insights (n.d.), for example, allows authors to do so on the following conditions:

- The author retains copyright to the preprint and developed works from it and is permitted to submit to the journal.
- The author declares that a preprint is available within the cover letter presented during submission. This must include a link to the location of the preprint.
- The author acknowledges that having a preprint publicly available means that the journal cannot guarantee anonymity of the author during the review process, even if they anonymise the submitted files.
- Should the submission be published, the authors are expected to update the information associated with the preprint version to show that a final version has been published in the journal, including the DOI linking directly to the publication.

Furthermore, the author guidelines should be carefully reviewed when selecting a journal, as they can be restrictive for some. For example, some journals have strict word-counts and some do not allow notes or endnotes at all. An author should seek a different venue if these components are important for developing and delivering a manuscript. Once a journal has been identified as a potential venue, the author guidelines should be reviewed when preparing a manuscript and before submission. Manuscripts that do not follow the guidelines can sometimes be desk-rejected. The author guidelines indicate the expected structure and format that follow a journal's house style. They can include, but are not limited to, the following components:

- file format: text, images and tables
- article length and word-count
- abstract or structured abstract

- article classification, e.g. research paper, conceptual paper, book review, communication
- headings and subheadings
- notes and endnotes
- references and referencing styles.

Predatory journals

Among the increasing number of journals, some are characterised as 'predatory'. A consensus definition (Grudniewicz et al., 2019) is:

> Predatory journals and publishers are entities that prioritize self-interest at the expense of scholarship and are characterized by false or misleading information, deviation from best editorial and publication practices, a lack of transparency and/or the use of aggressive and indiscriminate solicitation practices.

Elmore and Weston (2022) list the common characteristics of predatory journals as follows:

- claims to be a peer-reviewed open access publication but does not provide adequate peer review or the level of peer review promised
- advertises a journal impact factor or other citation metric on the website that is incorrect or cannot be verified
- may advertise an unrealistic timeline for publication
- publishes all articles for which authors pay an APC even if the article is low-quality, unrelated to the topic of the journal, or nonsensical
- publishes articles that have many grammatical mistakes, with little or no copyediting
- editorial board includes people who do not exist, do not have credentials relevant to the topic of the journal, have affiliations that cannot be verified, or are real people who are not aware that they are listed as members
- mimics name or website of other well-known, legitimate journals
- aggressively targets potential authors through e-mails
- may state that offices are in one country but contact details are in another
- solicitation e-mails contain grammatical errors of phishing scams
- lack of transparency about acceptance process or APC, so that authors do not know how much they will be charged until their article is accepted
- requires authors sign away their copyright to the article at the time of submission, making it impossible for the author to submit the article to another publisher

- publishes articles submitted before the authors have signed the publishing agreement, then refuses to take the article down if the author withdraws the submission
- removes articles or entire journals from the web without warning or informing authors.

The *Principles of Transparency and Best Practices in Scholarly Publishing* (COPE, DOAJ, OASPA and WAME, 2022) have been developed by the Committee on Publication Ethics (COPE), the Directory of Open Access Journals (DOAJ), the Open Access Scholarly Association (OASPA) and the World Association of Medical Editors (WAME). They can be used to detect if a journal or a publisher may be predatory by examining the following areas:

- journal content: name of journal, website, publishing schedule, archiving, copyright, licensing
- journal practices: publication ethics and related policies, peer review, access
- organisation: ownership and management, advisory body, editorial team
- business practices: author fees, other revenue, advertising, direct marketing.

Researchers are advised to be aware of the practices of predatory journals and avoid publishing in them. Predatory journals do not have the best interests of researchers or scholarship in mind but generate revenues by preying on researchers who are under pressure to publish. Think.Check.Submit (https://thinkchecksubmit.org) can help identify trusted publishers.

Conference proceedings

Conference submissions can include full research papers, short research papers, posters and panels. Proceedings are not considered as important as journal articles or monographs in formal research assessments in most disciplines, but they are important contributions in scholarly communication. Conferences are venues for researchers to share their work and work-in-progress and interact with their scholarly networks. In applied sciences and engineering disciplines, conference proceedings are often considered significant compared to other publication types because of the value placed on incremental contributions as building blocks of scientific progress.

The various types of conference submission are generally characterised as follows. Full research papers are reports of completed research and are most similar to journal articles but they tend to be shorter in length. Short research papers are reports of work-in-progress or preliminary findings; they are usually presented to solicit feedback from peers. Posters are graphical presentations that communicate a research study in a conversational style with conference participants; posters can also be posted on open research platforms to engage with a wider audience. Lastly, panel discussions are for panellists to offer their perspectives on an important topic or issue based on their expertise; in other words, panels are not organised for presenting original research, but to stimulate conversations and debates.

When submitting to a conference, a researcher will consider criteria similar to those of a journal: what are the aims and scope of the conference? What is the peer-review process? A researcher can also consider if the participants of the conference are peers they would like to get feedback from and collaborate with. Generally speaking, conference submissions do not go through a revision process: the conference organiser will make a decision to accept or reject based on the peer reviewers' recommendations. While some conferences implement a rebuttal process, it is not a common practice.

A researcher may ask 'Should I submit a conference paper if I plan to publish a full article in a journal at a later stage?' First, the researcher should check the journal policy. Some journals do not publish materials that have been previously published, meaning that an article cannot contain anything that has been included in a conference paper. Some journals are open to accepting submissions if a conference paper has been substantially expanded and revised. It is advisable to contact the editor(s) of a journal when submitting an article if it contains materials from a conference paper, to avoid problems of 'self-plagiarism' (see Chapter 8) or similar. Relatedly, a researcher should also be familiar with the copyright and publishing rights (see Chapter 4) of a conference proceeding. If the conference proceedings require transfer of copyright or exclusive licence to publish, then the conference paper cannot be republished in a different journal.

Non-traditional publication channels

New forms of academic publishing have emerged with the increased use of online platforms. While traditional publications in monographs and journals remain the most important in disseminating and sharing scholarly works, non-traditional publications (or research outputs) are increasingly used to publicise new publications, to engage with a wider audience and to enhance research and societal impacts. Researchers are encouraged to make use of these non-traditional publication channels during pre- and post-publication stages of their academic work.

Preprints

Preprints can be the submitted or accepted version of an article. A submitted version means that the manuscript has not gone through the peer-review process and that the methodologies and research findings have not been verified and vetted. The accepted version, commonly known as the author accepted manuscript (AAM), of an article is the final draft of an article that has been accepted for publication, that is, before the copyediting and typesetting process. On some platforms, multiple versions of a manuscript can be uploaded. Some authors prefer to share their findings immediately after a manuscript has been submitted, while others deposit the AAM after it has been accepted for publication in a journal.

Why do researchers deposit their articles on preprint servers? Preprints are most popular amongst researchers in the STEM disciplines, where rapid dissemination and exchange of research results are essential: they can reduce duplication of research that has been proven unyielding while encouraging replication when appropriate. Authors can also share data, codes and research results and receive feedback without the delays of the formal editorial and peer-review process. Preprints can also serve as a record or register of research studies/results when disputes occur. Those are the main reasons for researchers to share their manuscript on preprint servers, sometimes even before submission to a journal. In other words, the functionalities and availability of digital platforms have enabled preprints as a medium of scholarly communication. The first preprint server, ArXiv.org, was founded in 1991 and many preprint servers have since been established in STEM and social sciences disciplines.

In recent years there have been an increasing number of preprint servers and open research platforms for uploading preprints and other research outputs, including data, codes, slides, white papers, reports and so on. Some platforms are discipline-specific (e.g. medRxiv), while some have a broader scope (e.g. socArXiv). The functionalities (e.g. comments, versions) and the choices of publishing licences vary. Here are a few examples of domain-specific preprint servers:

- **medRxiv** The preprint server for health sciences, www.medrxiv.org.
- **MediArXiv** Open archive for media, film and communication studies, https://mediarxiv.org.
- **SocArXiv** Open archive of the social sciences, https://socopen.org.

The uploading of AAMs is to allow for wider dissemination of an article, particularly when the access to the version of record (VoR) requires a journal subscription or an article fee. Some journals allow the author(s) to upload the

AAM as soon as an article has been accepted, while for others the author(s) are required to wait until after the VoR has been published or even after an embargo period. Authors should consult the journal's open access policy before posting their manuscripts. Whether uploading a submitted version, AAM, or work-in-progress, it is also important to select the correct licensing option (see Chapter 4).

What is a version of record (VoR)?
Source: *The State of the Version of Record* by Lisa Janicke Hinchliffe (2022)
The version of record (VoR) is defined formally by industry organisations such as Crossref and NISO (National Information Standards Organization), and is sometimes colloquially referred to as 'the publisher PDF' or simply 'the PDF'.
Crossref: The typeset, copyedited and published version. It is stated that version control is important for traceability, identifiability, clarity, reduced replication and reduced errors.
NISO: a fixed version of a journal article that has been made available by any organization that acts as a publisher by formally and exclusively declaring the articles 'published'.

Blogs

Blogs can be used to communicate published research findings, work-in-progress or opinions on current issues for research and professional communities, as well as the mass media and the general public. They are alternative channels for researchers to engage in discussions about a topic of interest, or to increase the visibility of a journal article or a book by offering a summary in an accessible language. Blogs tend to be short pieces that range from 800 to 2,500 words and are written in a journalistic style utilising short paragraphs. Hyperlinks are used instead of a list of references for pointing to relevant scholarly publications and other supporting materials. Acronyms, academic terms and jargon are avoided where possible.

Blogs are often maintained and contributed by professional organisations, research groups and centres, or individual researchers. Some are used primarily for scholarly communication to engage the wider research community: a blog can provide updates and news about publications and events, as well as thought-provoking pieces about a current topic. Some researchers make use of the genre to develop ideas, converse and network with the research community. Two of the most widely read and shared blogs in scholarly communication are the LSE Impact Blog (LSE Impact Blog, n.d.) and Scholarly Kitchen (Scholarly Kitchen, n.d.). The former invites contributions from the scholarly community and the latter is contributed by a group of researchers and professors with occasional guest posts. The editors or moderators of a blog decide whether a contribution is relevant and appropriate and they also work with the author(s) on the title, contents, style and tone.

Blogs can also be used for science communication, public engagement and evidence-for-policy. Platforms with a subscription option are a good way to alert readers of new contents. Researchers can also publicise their contributions using social media. In addition to blogs, many newspapers and magazines also welcome journalistic pieces based on academic research, especially when the topic is of general interest. *The Conversation* (https://theconversation.com), for example, is a news site of articles primarily contributed by academic experts and RTÉ Brainstorm (www.rte.ie/brainstorm) is part of a newspaper.

Examples of blogs in the area of scholarly communication include:

- **Bibliomagician** Comments and practical guide for the LIS-Bibliometrics community, https://thebibliomagician.wordpress.com.
- **Björn Brembs** A personal blog on scholarly publishing, http://bjoern.brembs.net.
- **LSE Impact Blog** A platform for understanding and increasing the impact of academic research, https://blogs.lse.ac.uk/impactofsocialsciences.
- **Scholarly Kitchen** Official blog of the Society for Scholarly Publishing, https://scholarlykitchen.sspnet.org.

Podcasts and videocasts

Podcasts have become a popular medium to reach a wide audience in science communication and public engagement. Many podcasts are produced and hosted by learned societies and research hubs and they are advertised and shared on blogs and social media platforms. Podcasts are usually conversational and casual compared to a research seminar, where researchers can talk about a recent book or a topic of interest. Researchers can also be invited to contribute to podcasts for a general audience on topics of interest (e.g. LRB, The New Yorker, 99% Invisible, etc.) Interested audiences can listen to them anywhere with an internet connection and anytime. In addition, audio versions of blog posts and articles can also be recorded for wider dissemination; they are also accessible options for readers with visual impairment or dyslexia. Here are a few examples of podcasts of general and topical interests for researchers:

- **Science for Policy** podcast hosted by SAPEA (Science Advice for Policy by European Academies), https://sapea.info/podcast.

- The **Academic Freedom** podcast hosted by the Academic Freedom Alliance, https://academicfreedom.org/podcasts.
- **Uncommon Sense** hosted by *The Sociological Review*, https://thesociologicalreview.org/podcasts/uncommon-sense.
- **A History of Xenophobia** hosted by The History Hub, http://historyhub.ie/history-xenophobia.

Similarly, videocasts have also become common for sharing recordings of conference presentations and educational resources. They are useful resources, especially for those who are affected by travel restrictions, professional commitments and care responsibilities. Some researchers have also explored using animation and short documentaries for science communication and public engagement. An excellent example is the YouTube channel maintained by the research project PERITIA – Policy, Expertise and Trust. The channel includes public lectures, conference and workshop recordings and the winning Youth on Trust Awards, from experts who talk about their research in an accessible manner to videos made by students across Europe to share their view on the topic of trust in social and political life.

Publication types and scholarly communication

Monographs, journal articles, conference papers and posters, preprints, blogs and podcasts serve different purposes and audiences. Monographs are the most common form of publication in the arts and humanities and humanistic social sciences, for they offer the space for developing a thesis or argument. It takes a long period of time to write a monograph and it also takes time to read. Monographs and edited volumes tend to be scholarly works in long form and they are not suitable for rapid dissemination of research findings. Some scholars opt to write crossovers or trade books that appeal to the general audience, which is especially common in history and related disciplines. Journal articles are the most common form of scholarly publications in STEM disciplines and the applied social sciences. They are shorter in length with a faster turnaround time. Most are indexed on major databases and their citations are counted towards research assessment tools and platforms. Conference papers and posters are ideal for presenting work-in-progress and soliciting feedback, whereas non-traditional publications can be used to promote publications and engage the public audience. Each of the publication types offers opportunities for scholarly communication at a different pace and with a different audience.

In the work of research support, consultation services on publication types and the publishing process can sometimes be overlooked. For decades, researchers and scholars have been guided by the epistemic norms and tradition in their discipline when considering publication venues, while most are driven to publish in high-impact journals and with prestigious publishers in accordance with research assessment criteria. Yet researchers are not knowledgeable about the many options offered by journals and publishers when it comes to preparing for a book proposal, or spotting a potentially predatory journal, or the importance of reviewing the editorial and journal policy. The many considerations when choosing where to publish are complicated by the rapid changes in the scholarly communication landscape, involving open access and licensing options, the uses of research metrics and the increasing demand for societal and policy impact. Each of these topics will be discussed in more detail in the following chapters.

3
Open Access

Introduction
The open access movement was initiated when the internet became more widely available in the 1990s. It was envisioned that research findings and publications would be disseminated and shared freely online and that paywalls would be removed for public access to information. Over the decades, there has been a drastic increase in open access publications; however, full open access has not been achieved. The reasons are complex, involving the business models of commercial publishers, the perceived quality of open access publications and the criteria of research assessments. In recent years, researchers have been encouraged to publish their work in open access publications to increase reach and visibility and many libraries and consortia have negotiated transformative (also known as 'transitional' and 'read and publish') agreements with publishers. There emerge many ways of making a publication open access, as green, gold and diamond open access enter into the vernacular of scholarly publishing. These different open access models and their implications for the open access movement and scholarly communication are topics of ongoing discussions amongst research communities, librarians, research managers and funding agencies. From an author's perspective, it is essential to understand the pros and cons of the different open access models in relation to the potential dissemination and impact of their work and their influences on global knowledge production and the development of open research infrastructures.

The open access movement
The open access movement is usually traced to the three influential statements published in the early 2000s. The Budapest Open Access Initiative (BOAI), first published in 2002, defines open access (OA) as:

> the free availability [of literature] on the public internet, permitting any users to read, download, copy, distribute, print, search, or link to the full texts of these articles, crawl them for indexing, pass them as data to software, or use them for

any other lawful purpose, without financial, legal, or technical barriers other than those inseparable from gaining access to the internet itself.

(BOAI, 2002)

The Bethesda Statement on Open Access Publishing (June 2003) and the Berlin Declaration on Open Access to Knowledge in the Sciences and Humanities (October 2003) state that for a work to be OA, the copyright holder must consent in advance to let users 'copy, use, distribute, transmit and display the work publicly and to make and distribute derivative works, in any digital medium for any responsible purpose, subject to proper attribution of authorship' (Suber, 2012, 8).

The three statements are often referred to as the BBB definition of OA.

The internet was an incubator for the open access movement because scholarly publications can be 'free' from the confines of libraries and research institutions. The accessibility of the internet means that publications can be disseminated and distributed using online platforms and allow for free and open access. At the same time, it was hoped that OA scholarly publications could counter the 'serials crisis' – a term that describes the budgetary crisis due to the combination of exponential growth of journals and increasing subscription fees, often at a rate higher than inflation. Another strong argument for OA is that research results are largely publicly funded and hence should be publicly available and reusable. It was envisaged that the internet would provide the technological infrastructure for open access to information and scholarly communication.

Yet, the development of OA has not been as straightforward as envisaged in the BBB statements. Commercial publishers have long held important functions in the knowledge production system (Csiszar, 2018). In particular, the dominant market share of the so-called 'Big Deals' (see Chapter 9) and the significance of high-impact journals in research assessments (see Chapter 6) meant that academic publishing could not pivot to digital publishing in a blink of an eye without devising new business models. Despite the prospect of open access in the internet age, open access articles, journals and monographs are still not the default mode of academic publishing since the Declaration of BOAI over 20 years ago. Currently, there are three major open access models: Green, Diamond and Gold. The following sections provide an overview of each model and discuss the pros and cons from an author's point of view.

Green open access

Green open access refers to the self-archiving of a manuscript, that is, depositing an earlier version of a manuscript (not the VoR) in institutional repositories and/or making it available on personal websites and preprint servers. Depending on the journal policy, an author can deposit the author accepted manuscript (AAM) or earlier versions of the article with a citation to the published version. The AAM is the final version of an article before production processes such as copyediting and typesetting are carried out by the publisher. In most cases, the AAM can only be made openly accessible after an article has been formally published. However, some publishers impose an embargo period on green open access, meaning that the AAM cannot be made publicly available for a period of time, usually ranging from one to three years. For example, if a journal's open access policy indicates a two-year embargo period, then the author can only make the AAM openly accessible two years after the article has been published. During the embargo period, the article can only be accessible to those with a subscription.

Green open access allows a published article to be read by those who are kept out of the paywall, for example, independent researchers who are not affiliated with a university and researchers affiliated with libraries and universities with lower budgets. Green open access does not incur article processing charges (APCs). An author is not liable to pay APC and readers can access the submitted version or AAM freely available online. From a publisher's point of view, the green open access model is viable for independent, non-profit, library and learned society publishers who cannot afford to switch to the diamond open access model because their operations are supported by subscriptions or member fees.

An author can find out if green open access is an option by consulting the journal open access policy. Here are some examples:

1 University of Toronto Press: Authors whose research has been funded by a national, regional or international research funder may deposit a copy of the accepted manuscript (i.e. pre-copyediting, pre-typesetting, pre-tagging, but post-peer review) in an institutional repository twelve (12) months after publication of the version of record. (University of Toronto Press, 2022)
2 Emerald Publishing: Our green open access route offers all Emerald journal authors or book chapter authors the option to make their research immediately and openly available upon official publication, free from payment. You may deposit your author accepted manuscript at any point, but it must not be made publicly accessible until official publication. (Emerald Group, 2022)
3 Wiley Publishing: Self-archiving allows non-final versions to be hosted on a personal or institutional website. Submitted versions may be archived

immediately and accepted versions after an embargo period. (Wiley Publishing, 2022)

Self-archiving: institutional repositories and open research platforms
Institutional repositories are designed and developed for the collection and preservation of research outputs in a research institution, maintained and managed by the library. When a researcher uploads an article, intellectual property rights and embargo periods are checked and verified before a manuscript is made openly accessible. Items are assigned a unique identifier: a permanent URI (Uniform Resource Identifier), URL (Uniform Resource Locator) or a DOI (Digital Object Identifier). In addition to articles, institutional repositories also collect and preserve research outputs including reports, white papers, policy briefs and so on. The unique identifiers of the deposited items can be linked to researchers' profiles and they can also be located using search engines.

Open research platforms, including preprint servers, are increasingly common for sharing preliminary research findings and research outputs such as presentation slides, posters, codes and datasets. Some platforms are run by non-profit groups and organisations, while commercial platforms have also emerged in recent years. Authors (or creators) are responsible for resolving any copyright and publishing rights issues and selecting appropriate licences when using these platforms (see Chapter 4). Here are some examples of open repositories where researchers can deposit their manuscripts and other research-related materials:

- **Cambridge Open Engage** Cambridge Open Engage is the early and open content platform from Cambridge University Press, providing the space and resources for researchers to connect, collaborate and rapidly disseminate early and open research in various formats. www.cambridge.org/engage/coe/public-dashboard.
- **OSF (Open Science Framework)** The OSF platform includes OSF Preprints and OSF Registries. https://osf.io.
- **Zenodo** Zenodo was first launched in May 2013 to support the open access and open data movement, initially built and developed by researchers as a repository for European Commission funded research. It is now open to all. https://zenodo.org.

Diamond open access
Diamond open access (also known as platinum open access) refers to open access publications that are free to both authors and readers. They are free to

read and free to publish with no subscription fees or APCs. Diamond open access is an ideal open access model to make publications accessible in an open and fair manner: it alleviates the budgetary pressures faced by libraries while incurring no financial costs to authors and readers. In addition, many diamond open access journals are published by non-profit publishers that align with the interests and mission of scholarly communities. To a large extent, it is the model that matches the goals and objectives of the open access movement. Diamond open access publications are usually financially supported by associations, learned societies, libraries and universities. Here are a few examples:

- The *Journal of Electronic Publishing* (JEP) is an open access journal supported by the University of Michigan. JEP does not charge author processing charges or submission fees. The contents are freely available for anyone who is connected to the internet, while authors grant a non-exclusive publishing right (see Chapter 4) to the journal for publication and distribution.
- *Information Research* is an open access journal founded and edited by Professor Tom Wilson. It is currently published by the University of Borås, Sweden and funded by a Swedish Research Council scientific journal grant, with technical support by Lund University Libraries, Sweden.
- *Quantitative Science Studies* (QSS) is the official open access journal of the International Society for Scientometrics and Informetrics (ISSI), published by The MIT Press. The editors and editorial board members of the journal previously held editorial positions at the *Journal of Informetrics*, from which they resigned in early 2019 and established QSS in support of diamond open access (Sugimoto, 2019).

Diamond open access allows everyone to read an article immediately after it has been published. The VoR can be shared and accessed freely online and on most platforms they can be downloaded in PDF or EPUB format. The benefits of publishing in diamond open access publications are significant for making both publication and reading accessible to all. However, there are some barriers for researchers to support diamond open access journals, as in some disciplines they are perceived to be of lower quality because the publications are not indexed on WoS or Scopus. Nevertheless, the open research culture is increasingly endorsed by funding agencies and research institutions and publications in diamond open access publications will receive more support and recognition.

Gold open access

In gold open access publications, journal articles or monographs are made openly accessible when an author or their affiliated institution pays an article processing charge (APC). Some journals are gold open access only, meaning that all articles are open access and are subject to APC. Some journals are hybrid with a gold open access option: these are journals that are subscription-based but authors can make their article open access if they pay an APC. Gold open access is different from green open access in that the published articles (i.e. version of record), and not only the submitted or AAM, are openly accessible, while it is different from diamond open access in that APCs or book publishing charges (BPCs) are incurred. Both gold and diamond open access articles or books are usually published under a Creative Commons (CC) licence (see Chapter 4).

In recent years, some libraries and consortia have entered transformative (or transitional) agreements with major publishers. These agreements cover both the cost of subscription fees and APCs (sometimes referred to as 'read and publish' or 'publish and read' agreements). These agreements are negotiated with individual publishers and the terms vary in different institutions due to budget constraints. For example, some institutions are availed of unlimited gold open access articles, while others impose a quota of open access articles each year. The ESAC Transformative Agreement Registry (ESAC, n.d.) provides a list of transformative agreements provided by contributing institutions. The OpenAPC platform (OpenAPC, n.d.) releases data sets on APCs by universities and research institutions.

Many hybrid journals are published by traditional commercial publishers. They tend to have an established reputation and are tracked and indexed by major indexing services. The visibility and reach of publications are guaranteed. Further, the number of downloads are usually higher for open access publications, which can lead to citation advantages. However, researchers should be aware of what are called 'predatory publishing' and sometimes 'predatory journals' that charge APCs but do not have a proper or rigorous editorial or peer-review process (see Chapter 2).

Before choosing a gold open access option, researchers can check if a journal is indexed in major databases such as DOAJ (Directory of Open Access Journals), Scopus or WoS (Web of Science). It is also important for researchers to ensure that the licensing options comply with funding mandates and their own preferences (see Chapter 4). In addition, an author will need to ensure that the APC is budgeted or supported by a research grant or institutional funding, or if an agreement is in place between their affiliated institution and the publisher. Gold open access is an attractive option because many hybrid journals are established with a track record, especially when funding is available. Nevertheless, the gold open access model heavily relies on major commercial publishers and some argue that the pay-to-publish model is antithetical to bibliodiversity and equality in scholarly publications globally. These issues will be further discussed in Chapter 9.

Open monographs

Open monographs are published by a wide variety of publishers, including traditional commercial publishers, non-profit independent publishers, university presses and also new university presses (NUP). Open monographs are primarily online, but a print on demand (PoD) option is usually available, whilst some also have print runs. To publish an open monograph, authors may be required to pay a book processing charge (BPC). Open monographs with no BPCs are usually supported by subsidised programmes such as library publishing and some are supported by the subscribe to open (S2O) model.

Neylon et al. (2021) summarise key benefits of open monographs as follows:

- a higher geographic diversity of usage and reaching more countries
- increased access and usage for underserved populations and low- or middle-income countries
- higher number of downloads and citations than non-OA books
- the number of anonymous downloads is generally around double that of logged downloads (i.e. those with institutional identification).

Currently, open monographs are not as common as open access journal articles, due to the costs associated with book production: BPCs are significantly higher than APCs. Monographs also demand stronger support in publishing infrastructure, production and distribution, especially for smaller-scale publishers (Adema and Moore, 2021). At the same time, researchers can be reluctant to publish open monographs, due to the perceived lack of prestige or quality control; also, researchers in the humanities and social sciences are less likely to acquire external funding. As such, the development of open monographs requires institutional support and initiatives. The MIT Press Direct to Open, for example, is a subscribe to open (S2O) business model that uses subscription payments by over 265 institutions. Such initiatives are mostly welcomed by libraries and researchers; however, there are concerns about a fair and sustainable contribution/subscription model, involving issues such as the transparency of contributions.

The benefits of open monographs are significant in terms of distribution and impact; however, the wide adoption of open monographs will require strong institutional and policy support. There is also a need to demystify the quality-control issues pertaining to open monographs. Initiatives such as Open Library of Humanities (www.openlibhums.org) are pioneers in promoting open access to humanities researchers and scholars.

Open access at a crossroads

The open access movement has reached an important milestone in recent years. The academic publishing industry is moving toward open access, partly due to funding mandates that enforce publicly funded research to be published open access with no embargo period (see, for example, White House, 2022). In Europe, Plan S is an initiative for open access publishing that has been adopted by some European funding agencies. It is clear that open access is considered both a necessity and a requirement for the common good.

However, many consider the predominance of commercial publishers and their gold open access model and transformative ('read and publish' or 'publish and read') agreements as setbacks of the open access movement. It is because, first and foremost, the gold open access model does not resolve budgetary issues, as library finances remain strained under transformative agreements. It is expected that these agreements will only become more costly, due to funding mandates and open research policy, especially when publications in prestigious journals are considered as an important factor in research assessment. It has been reported that subscription fees and/or article-processing charges (APCs) have increased at rates higher than inflation (Crawford, 2021).

Secondly, researchers who cannot afford APCs are prevented from publishing in gold open access journals. Researchers who are independent and on precarious contracts, as well as researchers affiliated with institutions with limited funding, including those in low- and medium-income countries, cannot make their research publicly accessible. Essentially, the gold open access model entails that some voices are amplified, while others are more marginalised.

Thirdly, small publishers, including learned societies and non-profit publishers, can be crowded out of the market because they lack the resources to manoeuvre and switch into a business model that supports open access publishing, while the big commercial publishers become even more dominant. Transformative agreements can also lead to a leaner library budget for small and fringe publishers, as well as monographs and other materials.

> **The Fair Access Principles (Fair Open Access, n.d.)**
> The journal has a transparent ownership structure and is controlled by and responsive to the scholarly community.
> Authors of articles in the journal retain copyright.
> All articles are published open access and an explicit open access licence is used.
> Submission and publication is not conditional in any way on the payment of a fee from the author or their employing institution, or on membership of an institution or society.
> Any fees paid on behalf of the journal to publishers are low, transparent and in proportion to the work carried out.

Meanwhile, the development of the diamond open access has not been as successful as hoped. Studies have reported that many diamond open access journals have disappeared over the past two decades, especially those in the humanities and social sciences (Laakso, Matthias and Jahn, 2021). Independent open access journals can also struggle to attract submissions due to their limited visibility, especially when early-career researchers are advised to publish in WoS- or Scopus-indexed journals or similar. Although the diamond open access model is an excellent option for authors, readers and the open access movements, it will require institutional changes and financial support to thrive.

In addition, concerns have been raised regarding the commercialisation and marketisation of academic publishing, bibliodiversity and the long-term sustainability of the gold open access model. The European Commission report, *Operationalising Open Research Europe as a Collective Publishing Enterprise* (European Commission and Johnson, 2022), has indicated the plan to transition to open source platforms for journal articles, monographs and other research outputs. There are also scholar-led and community-led publishers, including library publishing, who advocate a sustainable diamond open access model. Some of these issues will be further discussed in Chapter 9.

> **What is bibliodiversity?**
> Bibliodiversity is cultural diversity applied to the world of books. Echoing biodiversity, it refers to the critical diversity of products (books, scripts, e-books, apps and oral literature) made available to readers. Bibliodiversity is a complex self-sustaining system of storytelling, writing, publishing and other kinds of production of oral and written literature. The writers and producers are comparable to the inhabitants of an ecosystem. Bibliodiversity contributes to a thriving life of culture and a healthy eco-social system (L'Alliance internationale des éditeurs indépendants, quoted in Chan, 2019).

> Shearer et al. (2020) highlight four major barriers to bibliodiversity that should be taken into account in open access models:
>
> 1. dominance of English as the lingua franca
> 2. concentration of infrastructures and services
> 3. limited funding models
> 4. narrow focus on journal-based policy measures.
>
> The Jussieu Call for Open Science and Bibliodiversity (https://jussieucall.org/jussieu-call) advocates that 'priority should be given to business models that do not involve any payments, neither for authors to have their texts published nor for readers to access them. Many fair funding models exist and only require to be further developed and extended: institutional support, library contributions or subsidies, premium services, participatory funding or creation of open archives, etc.

Library publishing

Library publishing encompasses a wide range of publications and platforms, including grey literature, journals, monographs, research data, institutional repositories and digital libraries. It is defined by the Library Publishing Coalition as 'the set of activities led by college and university libraries to support the creation, dissemination and curation of scholarly, creative and/or educational works' and characterised by 'a preference for open access dissemination and willingness to embrace informal and experimental forms of scholarly communication and to challenge the status quo' (Okerson and Holzman, 2015).

Ma, Buggle and O'Neill (2023) suggest that library publishing can play an important role in maintaining the bibliodiversity of the knowledge production ecosystem. Library publishing programmes are developing globally, supported by organisations including the Library Publishing Coalition (LPC) and the International Federation of Library Associations (IFLA) Library Publishing Special Interest Group (SIG). There are currently 145 academic and research library publishing programmes listed in the LPC's Library Publishing Directory and the majority of library-published books and journals are indexed on the Directory of Open Access Journals (DOAJ) and Directory of Open Access Books (DOAB).

Library publishers can fill in the gap where traditional academic publishers do not fulfil the needs for dissemination due to high rejection rates, long production schedules, high production costs and the transfer of intellectual property rights (Royster, 2014). They can also support the publication of niche and esoteric work that is unlikely to find a market, while developing high-quality, peer-reviewed e-journals and monographs (Lippincott, 2016). The development of New University Press (NUP) with reallocation of library budget (Verbeke and Mesotten, 2022) and Open Textbook Initiative (Buist-Zhuk and Nieborg, 2022) are examples of library publishing as a model of diamond open access. Unsworth (2014) argues that the development of library publishing has implications for professional identity, the research ecosystem and the future of the open access movement.

Open access and scholarly communication

When choosing where to publish, the open access policy of a publisher is an important consideration. Although all open access options – green, gold and diamond – make publications publicly accessible, their cost, dissemination and influences on scholarly publishing differ. Authors or their affiliated institutions must be able to afford APCs to be able to use the gold open access option, whereas the diamond open access option demands financial support other than, or in addition to, commercial means, for they tend to be non-profit operations. In Brazil, the open access platform SciELO has been operating since 1998 and it is now in service in 16 countries in Latin America and Africa. The recent development of AmeliCA and African Journals Online (AJOL) shows that open access plays a vital role in scholarly communication. It is important for researchers and librarians to understand the differences and support initiatives that align with the scholarly values for open and sustainable access. The open access option selected can shape the scholarly communication landscape in the future.

The open access movement has evolved into open research (or 'open science', or 'open scholarship') that encompasses open data, open methodology and open peer review. Openness is generally embraced by research communities, libraries, universities and funders. However, there can be many different interpretations that are being discussed, contested and refined. The discussion of open peer review in Chapter 5 is an example that demonstrates the possible configurations and implications, not dissimilar to the green, gold and diamond open access models discussed in this chapter.

Online resources
- **African Journals Online (AJOL)** African Journals Online is the world's largest and pre-eminent platform of African-published scholarly journals. www.ajol.info/index.php/ajol.

- **AmeliCA: (Conocimiento Abierto para América Latina y el Sur Global)** AmeliCA is a communication infrastructure for scholarly publishing and open science. http://amelica.org/index.php/en/home.
- **COAR (Confederation of Open Access Repositories)** COAR is an international association that brings together individual repositories and repository networks in order to build capacity, align policies and practices and act as a global voice for the repository community. www.coar-repositories.org.
- **COPIM (Community-led Open Publication Infrastructures for Monographs)** COPIM is an international partnership of researchers, universities, librarians, open access book publishers and infrastructure providers. www.copim.ac.uk.
- **Directory of Open Access Books (DOAB)** DOAB is a community-driven discovery service that indexes and provides access to scholarly, peer-reviewed open access books and helps users to find trusted open access book publishers. www.doabooks.org.
- **Directory of Open Access Journals (DOAJ)** DOAJ is a unique and extensive index of diverse open access journals from around the world. https://doaj.org.
- **Fair Open Access Alliance** The Fair Open Access Alliance is an overarching organisation aimed at co-ordinating efforts toward sustainable open access scholarly publishing. www.fairopenaccess.org.
- **Library Publishing Coalition (LPC)** The LPC is an independent, community-led membership association of academic and research libraries and library consortia engaged in scholarly publishing. https://librarypublishing.org.
- **OAPEN (Open Access Publishing in European Networks)** OAPEN promotes and supports the transition to open access for academic books by providing open infrastructure services to stakeholders in scholarly communication. https://oapen.org.
- **Open Book Publishers** An independent Open Access publisher in the Humanities and Social Sciences in the UK. www.openbookpublishers.com.
- **Open Library of Humanities** The Open Library of Humanities (OLH) is an award-winning, academic-led, diamond open access publisher. www.openlibhums.org.
- **OPERAS (Open Scholarly Communication in the European Research Area for Social Sciences and Humanities)** OPERAS is the research Infrastructure supporting open scholarly communication in the social sciences and humanities (SSH) in the European Research Area. https://operas-eu.org.

- **Redalyc (Sistema de Información Científica Redalyc)** Redalyc is an indexing system that contains open access journals in Latin America. www.redalyc.org.
- **SPARC** SPARC is a non-profit advocacy organisation that supports systems for research and education that are open by default and equitable by design. https://sparcopen.org.
- **Think. Check. Submit.** Think. Check. Submit. helps researchers identify trusted journals and publishers for their research. https://thinkchecksubmit.org.

4
Copyright and Licence to Publish

Introduction
This chapter provides an overview of copyright, publishing rights and licensing options from an author's perspective. It serves as a guide to understanding some of the common terminologies an author may encounter in journal policies or publishing agreements and contracts. It also discusses the development of rights retention, especially in the context of open access (Chapter 3). It does not, however, cover copyright issues related to the use of materials such as fair use and it is not intended to provide legal advice. For a comprehensive guide of copyright in libraries, archives and information services, please refer to Graham Cornish's *Copyright: interpreting the law for libraries, archives and information services* (2019). In this chapter, we focus on the question: why should authors care about copyright, publishing rights and licensing options when they decide where to publish?

Copyright
What is copyright? According to the US Copyright Office, 'Copyright is a type of intellectual property that protects original works of authorship as soon as an author fixes the work in a tangible form of expression' (US Copyright Office, n.d.). Generally speaking, copyright prevents people from copying, distributing, renting or lending, performing, showing or making adaptations of your work, including putting it on the internet (www.gov.uk/copyright). In most countries, copyright lasts a minimum of life plus 50 years, however the duration is different in regions and for different media types.

In *Who Owns Academic Work*, McSherry (2001) states that facts, either natural or historical, cannot be copyrighted; however, expressions and interpretations can be copyrighted. Copyright protection is automatically granted to the authors or creators of original works. However, the copyright of scholarly works does not always belong to the authors. First, a university and research institution, as the employer, is the first owner of the copyright in the work in some cases, although most scholarly and pedagogical works can be exempted under the institution's intellectual property policy.

Secondly, authors may be requested to transfer copyright to the publisher when an article or a book is accepted for publication.

For many academic authors, the copyright question is overlooked because they do not expect monetary rewards when publishing in an academic journal or even a monograph. But should authors transfer copyright to the publisher? After the copyright has been transferred, an author no longer owns the article, meaning that they cannot sell, distribute or share the article. It also means that the copyright holder (i.e. the publisher) can sell, distribute and share the article as they wish, even when an author retains the moral right as the creator of the work. In other words, the author(s) cannot publish, share, or grant usage of their own work elsewhere such as a personal website or with a different publisher/journal after the copyright transfer. Vollmer succinctly explains:

> If an author transfers copyright, the author will often give the publisher full exclusive rights of reproduction, adaptation, distribution, public display and public performance. Essentially, an author who transfers copyright without retaining rights is put in a position where permission must be sought from the publisher for the author to use personally created work, unless the use falls under a limitation or exception to copyright, such as fair use. Another consequence of transferring the copyright to the publisher is the loss of the ability to share the work under a CC licence. The copyright holder is the only person who can attach a CC licence to a work.
>
> (Vollmer, 2022, 385)

Put another way, when a researcher who has transferred copyright talks about 'their' article, it is actually owned by the publisher. The transfer of copyright can be problematic for culturally sensitive materials that should be treated carefully in the process of distribution (i.e. should not be distributed or marketed in certain regions), adaptation and translation. It can also be problematic when a researcher wants to reuse supplementary materials such as survey questions in future studies because the publisher now owns the copyright of the survey.

In principle, the ownership of copyright can be negotiated before signing a book contract or publishing agreement. An author should find out details about copyright and licensing on the publisher's or journal's website before submitting a book proposal or article. Understandably, authors are reluctant to move to a different publisher or a journal after a manuscript has been accepted for publication. For example, here are two publishers who require copyright transfer or granting of exclusive licence to the copyright for publications in subscription journals (i.e. not open access) at the time of writing:

- **Elsevier**
  'For articles published under the subscription model, the authors typically transfer copyright to Elsevier. In some circumstances, authors may instead grant us (or the learned society for whom we publish) an exclusive licence to publish and disseminate their work.' (Elsevier, n.d.)
- **Wiley Author Services**
  'For subscription articles, you will either transfer copyright to Wiley with a Copyright Transfer Agreement (CTA) or grant Wiley an exclusive licence to the copyright with an Exclusive Licence Agreement (ELA). You will receive the appropriate licence agreement in the time between acceptance of your article and final publication online.' (Wiley Author Services, n.d.)

The requirement of copyright transfer or exclusive licence is common in scholarly publishing. From the perspective of the publisher, the practice protects their commercial interest, since copyright transfer or exclusive licence ensures that the publisher can derive revenues from the publications for their added-value services. A counterargument, however, is that publishers are already earning incomes from subscriptions or APCs that would have covered their costs in processing, producing and marketing. Further, copyright transfer means that whether an article can be open access is at the discretion of the publisher.

Licence to publish: exclusive and non-exclusive

What is an exclusive licence mentioned in the two examples above? Put simply, the licence allows the publisher to publish, communicate and distribute the publication exclusively even though an author retains the copyright. The exclusive licence protects the publisher for their value-added services in the production and publishing processes involving copyediting and typesetting. It is not much different from copyright transfer, except that an author can negotiate the duration of the exclusive licence to publish, meaning that an author can publish with a different publisher after the exclusive licence has expired. This is particularly important if a work is expected to be translated in other languages and/or adapted in documentaries and films. Sometimes an author may also opt to republish with another publisher for better publicity or royalties.

An author does not have the right to make an article open access (including uploading it on preprint servers and other services) or grant a Creative Commons licence if a publisher requires copyright transfer or an exclusive licence.

For publishers or journals that offer a green open access option, the publishing agreement should include terms and conditions for self-archiving of the author accepted manuscript (AAM). The information is usually available in the open access/research policies. For example, the publisher Emerald states that:

> you may deposit your author accepted manuscript at any point, but it must not be made publicly accessible until official publication (i.e. as soon as it appears on Emerald Insights in its final typeset version).
>
> (Emerald Group, 2022)

Some publishers do not offer a green open access option unless an article is under funding mandate. The UTP (University of Toronto Press) Journals' green open access policy states that:

> Authors whose research has been funded by a national, regional, or international research funder may deposit a copy of the accepted manuscript (i.e., pre-copyediting, pre-typesetting, pre-tagging, but post-peer review) in an institutional repository twelve (12) months after publication of the version of record. The deposit must include the article DOI linking out to the published version.
>
> (University of Toronto Press, 2022)

Not all publishers or journals require transfer of copyright or exclusive licence to publish. Some journals only require the granting of a non-exclusive licence to distribute and share the published articles or monographs. In other words, an author is free to publish and distribute their work on other platforms, in print or digitally. Non-exclusive publishing licences are common amongst diamond and some gold open access journals, for they do not depend on subscriptions as a source of revenue, although the open access option in and of itself does not exclude the possibility of copyright transfer or granting of exclusive licence. In other words, open access does not necessarily grant the right of reuse, redistribution or adaptation of the work, which can be offered by a Creative Commons licence.

An author can grant publishing rights – exclusive or non-exclusive – and Creative Commons licences as the copyright holder. It is an author's responsibility to select the most suitable and appropriate licences. A book author may want to limit the duration of exclusive publishing rights such that they can have the option to republish with a different publisher after a period of time. Funded authors will need to comply with funding mandates to publish their research findings on platforms that allow open access, reuse and replication. In these cases, the authors must select publications where they can retain copyright and grant a non-exclusive licence to publish.

It should also be noted that open access publishing is not the same as rights retention, although the two topics are often discussed together. Authors should actively seek information about copyright and publishing licences when they select publication venues. Open access publishing allows access; however, the control over the publication and distribution of published works is contingent on copyright and publishing licences. These requirements should be considered before submitting an article to a journal or a publisher, as these terms and conditions usually become non-negotiable when an article is accepted for publication or after a book contract has been signed.

Creative Commons (CC) licences

When publishing in open access journals and open monographs and when uploading preprints, slides, posters and other materials on digital platforms, authors and creators are often required to select a Creative Commons (CC) licence. These licences grant permissions for others to copy, distribute, edit, remix and build upon a piece of work within the boundaries of copyright law. Instead of 'all rights reserved', authors and creators can allow others to use and reuse their works with CC Licences.

The six licences as explained on the Creative Commons website (https://creativecommons.org/licences/?lang=en)

This licence lets others distribute, remix, adapt and build upon your work, even commercially, as long as they credit you for the original creation.

This licence lets others remix, adapt and build upon your work even for commercial purposes, as long as they credit you and license their new creations under the identical terms.

This licence lets others reuse the work for any purpose, including commercially; however, it cannot be shared with others in adapted form and credit must be provided to you.

This licence lets others remix, adapt and build upon your work non-commercially and although their new works must also acknowledge you and be non-commercial, they don't have to license their derivative works on the same terms.

This licence lets others remix, adapt and build upon your work non-commercially, as long as they credit you and license their new creations under the identical terms.

This licence is the most restrictive of our six main licences, only allowing others to download your works and share them with others as long as they credit you, but they can't change them in any way or use them commercially.

Publishers and online platforms offer different options when it comes to CC licences: for some, CC BY is the only option for open access publishing, while for others more options are available. From an author's perspective, here are some considerations:

CC BY – Granting a CC BY licence means that anyone can use, distribute and reuse your work as long as they attribute and credit the original work. In scholarly publications, attribution is mostly guaranteed in the sense that others will cite your work, while quoting extensively without citation would be considered plagiarism. When authors grant a CC BY licence, they cannot claim compensation if a third party sells copies of their work and/or uses it for other commercial purposes and they are happy with derivative works. The CC BY licence is mandated by some funding agencies/programmes.

CC BY-SA – While this licence allows for commercial and non-commercial uses, it requires that all new works based on the original work carry the same licence. In other words, if someone produces a derivative work, the derivative work must be assigned the same licence.

CC BY-ND – If an author does not allow derivative works, then the non-derivative licence would work well. The licence can also include the non-commercial element: CC BY-NC-ND, which would be the most restrictive of all CC licences.

CC BY-NC – If an author is fine with making their work accessible and reusable as long as it is for non-commercial use, then a CC BY-NC licence would be appropriate. This means that the author can claim compensation if someone uses the published work for commercial gain.

When selecting a CC licence, an author should consider how they want the published works to be distributed, adapted, used and reused for commercial or non-commercial purposes. These two questions can easily help with the selection (Creative Commons, n.d.):

1 Do you allow adaptations of your work?
   (a) Yes
   (b) No → add **ND**
   (c) Yes, as long as others share alike → add **SA**
2 Do you allow commercial uses of your work?
   (a) Yes
   (b) No → add **NC**

Again, an author must be the copyright holder to grant a CC licence. However, not all journals or publishers offer every licence as an option. For instance, some journals require that an article to be published under the CC BY licence only, while others offer options including CC BY-NC and CC BY-NC-ND. The availability of these options should be clarified before submission.

Rights retention strategy

> Authors who retain rights don't violate rights belonging to publishers; they merely prevent publishers from acquiring those rights in the first place.
>
> (Suber, 2012)

Rights retention strategies respond to the challenges posed by copyright transfer and exclusive publishing licences. The logic of open access applies: why are scholarly works and research results owned by publishers when they are supported by public funds? Many have argued that researchers should retain their rights to their work. Rights retention has implications for the development of open access because signing away the copyright or granting an exclusive licence means that a publisher can decide whether a piece of work can be accessible, openly or behind a paywall. Rumsey (2021) succinctly explains that 'LTPs [licences to publish] are presented as non-negotiable, "take-it-or-leave it" agreements. The publisher has put forth their demands in their terms. Once the author has signed, the publisher effectively takes full control of content which is not theirs.'

So, what can authors do to retain their rights? Eglen (2022), amongst others, suggests adding the following text to a manuscript before submission and then deposit the AAM without embargo in the institutional repository once the article has been accepted for publication:

> For the purpose of open access, the author has applied a CC BY public copyright licence to any Author Accepted Manuscript version arising from the submission.

This rights retention strategy means that the AAM will be openly accessible even though a green open access option is not available (see example of University of Toronto Press above). If a publisher does not accept the terms, then an editor can desk-reject the manuscript at the submission stage.

Rights retention strategies have been implemented or trialled by some institutions which require all researchers to deposit the AAM in the institutional repositories. However, it is still early to say whether the policy will become acceptable or commonplace.

Copyright, licences and scholarly communication

Questions and concerns pertaining to copyright and publishing licences are often overlooked. It is partly because of the status quo of traditional publishers: they have been asking for copyright transfer or the granting of exclusive licence to publish for decades and there have been no or few objections. It is partly because most researchers do not understand the terms and conditions when they sign a publishing agreement, as the publication requirement in research assessment is their main concern. Many are bewildered by the various CC licences, not knowing which one to choose.

Copyright and publishing licences come into the spotlight in the development of open access and open research – for there is no guarantee that publications and other research outputs will be openly accessible when they are owned by the publishers and other entities. The UNESCO Recommendation on Open Science (UNESCO, 2021) has recommended that '[A]ny transfer or licensing of copyrights to third parties should not restrict the public's right to immediate open access to scientific publication' (para 7a). There are calls for copyright reform (Willinsky, 2022) and rights retention strategy by advocacy groups such as SPARC and cOAlition S. ALLEA (All European Academies) has also issued a statement that supports rights retention and further changes in copyright law, indicating developments in EU countries including the 2019 Directive on Copyright in the Digital Single Market and the Secondary Publication Rights (ALLEA, 2022)'.

This chapter provides some signposts in the consideration of copyright and licensing options. They can be used to navigate scholarly publishing, especially because rights retention is elemental in the progress of open access. These copyright and related intellectual property issues will become more prominent in the discussion of open data and other research outputs (European Commission and and Senftleben, 2022). The work of research support and scholarly communication does not involve offering legal advice, but it is essential to keep abreast of the implication of copyright and licensing issues on scholarly publishing and communication.

Online resources
- **Sherpa Romeo** Sherpa Romeo is an online resource that aggregates and analyses publisher open access policies from around the world and provides summaries of publisher copyright and open access archiving policies on a journal-by-journal basis. https://v2.sherpa.ac.uk/romeo.
- **Plan S Rights Retention Strategy** Summary and case study of rights retention strategy. www.coalition-s.org/rights-retention-strategy.

- **The Rights Retention Strategy** HTML slides provided by Stephen J. Eglen (CC BY 4.0). https://sje30.github.io/talks/2022/rrs-cam.html.

5
Peer Review

Introduction

Peer review is a process by which the quality, novelty and originality of scholarly works are assessed and appraised. It is an established mechanism in making decisions about the acceptance and rejection of manuscripts. As such, it also serves as a form of quality control in scholarly publishing: a peer reviewed article is a manuscript that has been vetted by subject experts in the research area. In the guidelines for good practice, Hames (2007, 2–3) suggests that peer review performs the following functions:

1. prevent the publication of bad work and filter out studies that have been poorly conceived, designed or executed
2. check that the research reported has been carried out well and there are no flaws in the design or methodology
3. ensure that the work is reported correctly and unambiguously, with acknowledgment to the existing body of work
4. ensure that the results presented have been interpreted correctly and all possible interpretations considered
5. ensure that the results are not too preliminary or too speculative, but at the same time not block innovative new research and theories
6. select work that will be of the greatest interest to the readership
7. provide editors with evidence to make judgements as to whether articles meet the selection criteria for their particular publications
8. generally improve the quality and readability of a publication.

Why should an author consider the peer-review process when choosing where to publish? It is because the peer-review process can vary for different publication types and for different publishers. It is important for an author to consider the peer-review process before submission because there are advantages and disadvantages associated with the process, depending on the author's career stage, the speed of publication and the thoroughness and openness of peer reviews. For conference proceedings and journal articles, double- and single-blind peer reviews are the most common, while open peer review and post-publication peer review have been proposed and adopted in recent years. For monographs and edited books, the peer-review process can vary from the book proposal stage to the final manuscript. Understanding the peer-review process is essential when preparing a manuscript or book proposal.

The peer-review process

The peer-review process begins with the selection of peer reviewers. Ideally, the reviewers are peers who are familiar with the theories, methodologies and methods in a subject area. In the peer-review process, they are to comment on whether the literature review is thorough, the methodologies and methods are appropriate, the discussions and conclusions are substantiated by findings and claims are justified. Peer reviewers are selected based on their subject expertise, which can be discerned by their publications and conference presentations. The key role of peer reviewers is to make recommendations – whether an article should be published – while they also provide constructive feedback for improving the quality of manuscripts.

The peer-review criteria are not always explicitly stated. For some journals, reviewers are asked to respond to specific questions, whilst others are more open-ended. Figures 5.1, 5.2 and 5.3 are examples of peer review forms. Peer reviewers are asked to provide feedback that they can type in a text box or upload as a document, including general comments and suggestions for improving and revising an article and sometimes the reasons for rejecting a manuscript. Some journals provide guidelines for reviewers (Figure 5.2) and some require peer reviewers to respond to specific questions/criteria (Figure 5.3).

Recommendations
☐ Accept
☐ Accept with revisions
☐ Revise and Resubmit
☐ Reject
Confidential Comments to the Editor
Comments to the Author

Figure 5.1 *Peer review form: Example 1 (no specific questions)*

Reviewer Guidelines
- Is the paper technically competent? Are the arguments, facts, logic, sources, all reasonable? Can you understand it all?
- Is it interesting, stimulating and of general interest to the research evaluation community (broadly defined)?

- Any unfortunate gaps?
- If it claims originality, is that claim plausible?
- Are all the tables and illustrations helpful?
- Is it clear what methodology has been used and is the methodology sound? We strongly encourage reviewers to raise queries with the editors over any uncertainties over methodology.
- Does the paper demonstrate a clear fit within the journal and its scope? Manuscripts should focus directly on research evaluation theory and/or practice. For papers examining dynamic or outcomes of research processes/activities, implications for research evaluation should be clear.

Your comments will be shared with the author(s) without revealing your identity. Your recommendation and any comments designated for the Editor only will not be shared.

*Recommendations
☐ Accept
☐ Minor Revision
☐ Major Revision
☐ Reject
Confidential Comments to the Editors
*Comments to the Author

Figure 5.2 *Peer review form: Example 2 (with specific questions)*

Does this article present the novel progress of any primary research, practice, application, service and technology?

☐ Excellent
☐ Good
☐ Average
☐ Poor

Have the experiment, statistics and any analysis in this article been performed appropriately and rigorously and been described in sufficient detail?

☐ Yes
☐ No

Are the discussion and conclusion part in this article presented in an appropriate fashion and supported by the data?

☐ Yes
☐ No

Is the article presented in an intelligible fashion and written in Standard English?

☐ Yes
☐ No

Recommendation
☐ Accept
☐ Minor Revision
☐ Major Revision
☐ Reject
Confidential Comments to the Editor
Comments to the Author

Figure 5.3 *Peer review form: Example 3 (with specific questions)*

The peer-review process: journal articles

Before getting into the peer-review process, it would be helpful to understand what happens after a manuscript has been submitted – it does not go to the peer reviewers right away! Generally speaking, the editor(s) will first examine whether the submitted manuscript is within the scope and meets the quality standard of the journal. If a manuscript does not meet the basic criteria, the editor(s) will respond with a desk reject, meaning that the manuscript will not go through the peer-review process. It is an important step in the editorial process: it is advantageous for the author(s) because they can revise the manuscript or submit their manuscript to a more suitable journal without the lengthy wait; it also alleviates the workload of peer reviewers.

If a manuscript fits the scope and meets the basic requirements for a journal, then the editor(s) will seek peer reviewers to provide feedback and recommendations for the manuscript. Each manuscript is usually reviewed by two or three reviewers. In addition to expertise and experience, peer reviewers are also selected to reflect different epistemological positions, perspectives and specialisations in methods and methodologies. The peer-review process can take months and sometimes over a year, depending on the volume of submissions and the availability of peer reviewers. Once all invited peer reviewers have submitted their reviews, the editor(s) will take into consideration their recommendations and comments before making a decision. If the peer reviewers' recommendations do not agree, for example, one reviewer recommends rejection and another reviewer provides strong reasons for acceptance, then the editor(s) will usually seek a third or fourth reviewer for recommendation before making a decision, which can be: accept, accept with revisions (or minor revisions), revise and resubmit (major revisions) and reject. Manuscripts usually go through one or two rounds of revisions before they are accepted for publication.

The length of the peer-review process can be an important factor when considering where to publish. Early-career researchers tend to prefer publications with a faster turnaround time because a prolonged peer-review process can mean missing a job opportunity due to the lack of publications when they are looking for academic positions. Research findings on an emerging phenomenon can be outdated with a protracted peer-review process. It is an essential step to look up the information about the peer-review process when selecting a publication channel. Journal websites usually indicate the expected turnaround time; it is appropriate to contact the editor-in-chief if the information is not publicly available. In reality, the peer-review process can be lengthened due to the unavailability of peer reviewers or delayed reviews and it can be shorter than expected when reviewers respond swiftly!

The peer-review process: conferences

The peer-review process of conferences is largely the same as that of journal articles with one significant difference: the conference programme chair(s) must make the decision to accept or reject upon receiving the peer-review scores. In most cases, it is not possible for the author(s) to make multiple revisions due to the fact that a conference is to be held on specific dates. Some conferences include a rebuttal process whereby the author(s) can respond to the peer reviewers' comments and make a case to the conference chair(s).

Since conferences can include work-in-progress papers/posters and panel submissions, the criteria for peer review can be different from a journal submission. For instance, panel submissions cannot be double-blind, as the composition of panel members is part of the evaluation, while peer review of work-in-progress papers/posters focuses on the novelty and originality of topics. In other words, conference submissions are not necessarily evaluated based on the significance of the research findings, but the relevance to the theme and the potential for discussions and debates.

The peer-review process: monographs and edited books

There are two stages in the peer review of monographs and edited books: (1) book proposal and (2) completed manuscript. A book proposal usually includes the synopsis and indicates the unique contributions and features of the manuscript, accompanied by a sample chapter. The proposal is usually reviewed by two to three subject experts regarding the originality and academic merits. Peer reviewers may also make suggestions for broadening or narrowing down the scope of a monograph. In addition, peer reviewers are also requested to comment on the proposed book's potential readership and marketability and to suggest competing titles and the geographical reach of the book. For edited books (or compilations), the contributors and their contributions are also assessed. Peer review at the proposal stage is typically single-blind.

Completed manuscripts aimed at professionals, students (textbooks) or general readers do not necessarily go through the peer-review process. For academic works, the completed manuscript will be peer-reviewed and the criteria are similar to those of journal publications: the manuscript should advance knowledge by providing new insights and interpretations and, if applicable, data collection and analysis are appropriate and rigorous and the presentation of findings is of great interest to the potential readers. Peer reviews of book manuscripts take two to three months and can be longer, depending on the length and complexity. The managing editor or the series editor will recommend and request changes and amendments based on the reviewers' comments and suggestions. A book manuscript under contract can still be rejected if the peer reviewers are not satisfied with its scope, contents or quality.

Traditional peer review

When considering where to publish, it is important to consider the editorial and peer-review process: Is a prolonged wait feasible for a researcher who is looking for a postdoc position or applying for a grant? Is the process fair and effective? Essentially, the peer-review process is not only about acceptance and rejection, but also providing constructive feedback for improving the manuscripts. Peer reviewers are also tasked with detecting fraudulent research, paper mill articles and plagiarism (Chapter 8). A robust peer-review process is an indicator of a reputable publication.

The type of peer review can also affect a researcher's choice of publication channel. Traditionally, single- and double-blind peer review are the most common and each has its pros and cons. An early-career researcher from a lesser-known institution can be disadvantaged if their identity is disclosed in the peer-review process, whereas identity checks can be helpful in detecting paper mill articles. From an author's perspective, the key concerns are the potential biases in peer review.

Double-blind peer review

Double-blind peer review means that the authors and peer reviewers do not know each other's identity in the peer-review process. When submitting an article, the authors are asked to remove their names and affiliations in the manuscript; sometimes it is also necessary to blind self-citations. The most important feature of double-blind peer review is its anonymity and the fairness and neutrality implied. That is to say, peer reviewers will assess a manuscript based on its contents: whether the methodology and methods are appropriate or novel, whether the contribution advances knowledge and whether the article will appeal to the audience of a journal. They do not assess the author(s) based on their affiliations, track records, or other personal characteristics such as gender, sexuality, or ethnicity.

Double-blind peer review is perceived as more equitable and most beneficial for researchers in their early career, as well as those in the so-called 'scientific periphery' or 'global south', because the process prevents identity-based and track record-based biases and discrimination. In other words, double-blind peer review means that the evaluation of a manuscript will not be affected by the names or affiliations of an author. A manuscript will not be judged better because an author is an established figure or shunned due to the perceived lack of prestige of an institution. From an author's perspective, double-blind peer review can be considerably beneficial for those who are in their early career and those who may be prejudiced against.

Single-blind peer review
In single-blind peer review, the identity of the author is disclosed to the reviewer, but the author does not know the identity of the reviewers. What are the benefits of single-blind peer review, considering the potential biases and discrimination avoided in double-blind peer review? One argument is that reviewers can provide constructive feedback based on their knowledge of the authors' previous works. Peer reviewers can also be more constructive in their feedback if they know the authors are early-career researchers. Yet, some argue that established authors can have an advantage, since peer reviewers may give credits based on their previous works or seniority. The key issue is whether the evaluation should be solely based on the manuscript under review and whether the track records or affiliations of the authors are relevant in the peer-review process.

Single-blind peer review can be useful in detecting research integrity issues (Chapter 8). The characteristics of paper mill articles, for example, include the lack of affiliations or the change of authorship. Hence, the disclosure of an author's identity is useful for exposing forged authorship. In other cases, the affiliated institutions may also provide some hints about potential fabrication of data or images based on the facilities and infrastructure.

Nevertheless, it is problematic when a manuscript is peer-reviewed by a competitor or a rival. What can an author do? On some submission platforms, authors can indicate individuals who should not be invited as peer reviewers of their manuscript. If the option is not available, authors can write to the editor and make a request.

Problems and issues of traditional peer review
Double- and single-blind peer reviews are not without problems and issues. In recent years, one of the biggest challenges is the so-called peer-review crisis in journal publishing (Publon, 2018; Flaherty, 2022). It has been reported that 10% of reviewers are responsible for 50% of all peer reviews, while 'more than 70% of researchers decline review requests because the article is outside of their area of expertise, 42% of them decline because they are too busy' (Petrescu and Krishen, 2022). The most significant issue of the peer-review crisis is the delayed feedback for authors and publications, which has led to discussions about 'crowdsourcing' peer reviews and the urgent need for peer-review training for potential reviewers in emerging regions outside of North

America and Europe. On the one hand, the peer-review crisis concerns the speed and quality of peer review. When potential reviewers are unavailable, the review of the manuscript will certainly be delayed; at times, an editor may need to reach out to potential reviewers who are not specialised in the topic or methodology. On the other hand, the peer-review crisis also poses questions about the incentives for and recognition of the work of peer review. The shortage of peer reviewers is partly due to the fact that they are volunteers, yet their contributions are usually not recognised or rewarded, not to mention that they are also under pressure to research and publish.

Furthermore, the traditional peer-review process is seen as a 'black box', as editors can select reviewers based on their known preference for topics and methodologies which can lead to issues of confirmation bias or conservatism. The situation can be acute when selected peer reviewers are risk-averse: for example, when some have strong preferences for existing theories and methodologies and are resistant to innovative methods or results. Confirmation bias also suggests the preference for positive over negative or neutral results, or replication studies (Johnson and Dickersin, 2007; Garcia, Rodriguez-Sánchez and Fedez-Valdivia, 2020). There are concerns about accountability, due to the fact that reviewers are anonymous and are not accountable for publications, notwithstanding that they hold the power as to whether an article is published or rejected. Furthermore, potential biases based on gender, institutional affiliation, language, nationality and so on can also be embedded in the peer-review process (Lee et al., 2013).

Accountability and transparency are of utmost importance in the peer-review process, without which the validity of and trust in research can be brought into question. Two types of peer review have been suggested to ensure and improve the peer-review process: open peer review and post-publication peer review, enabled by digital platforms that can facilitate participation by many peer reviewers.

Open peer review (OPR)

Open peer review (OPR) is an umbrella term which encompasses 'open' practices that aim to address the various problems and issues of traditional peer review. The black-box nature of peer review can be made more transparent by open identities; biases and conservatism can be moderated by open interactions and participation; and the peer review crisis can be tackled by incentivising and rewarding peer reviews by open reports. Open identities, open interactions, open participation and open reports are forms of open peer review that align with the values of open research or open scholarship. While these practices have been adapted and trialled, there is no single model of open peer review and there are ongoing discussions about the pros and cons of different approaches, particularly when considering disciplinary differences in the nature of research and scholarship. Open identities, open reports, open interaction and open participation are the most common practices in open peer review (Ross-Hellauer, 2017; PLOS, n.d.):

Open identities
The identities of authors and reviewers are disclosed to each other. The proponents of open identities argue that the practice can enhance accountability and transparency: when reviewers are not shielded from anonymity, they will be more open about potential conflict of interests and their evaluation will be fairer. However, some argue that reviewers may hold back on their opinions to avoid conflicts or offence, especially for early-career researchers who may be worried about repercussions in their career.

Open reports
The reviews are published alongside the published article. Since published articles do not necessarily address all concerns of the reviewers, open reports are beneficial for readers to consider the criticisms and reservations, or if any errors have been overlooked during the peer-review process. When the open reports are signed (open identity), then the reviewers are incentivised to make their work recognised. Open reports are also useful for early-career researchers as a guide to approach peer review.

Open interaction
Inconsistent or contradictory peer reviews prolong the revision process and can be frustrating for authors. Open interaction allows reciprocal discussion between reviewers and editors and/or between authors and reviewers during the peer-review process, which can resolve any disagreements before an editor issues the decision letter and reviewers' reports.

Open participation
A manuscript is reviewed by any interested member of the scholarly community. It is also known as crowdsourced peer review, community review or public review. These reviews are solicited where the manuscript is hosted, where reviewers can provide full reviews or short comments. On some platforms, reviewers' credentials are verified. In principle, open participation can resolve issues including biased selection of reviewers and increase reliability by increasing the number of reviewers. In practice, however, the approach has not been successfully implemented due to the relatively small number and varied qualities of reviews.

Open peer review aligns with the aims and values of open research, while it also addresses some problems and issues of traditional double- or single-blind peer review. So far, the practices of open peer review have mainly been adopted in medical and scientific disciplines, with a steady growth since 2001 (Horbach and Halffman, 2020; Wolfram et al., 2020). Interested readers can consult Ross-Hellauer and Görögh's (2019) proposed guidelines for implementing open peer review.

Post-publication peer review (PPPR)

Post-publication peer review (PPPR) is considered as a form of open peer review and sometimes referred to as 'open final version commenting' or similar. Markie (2015) suggests that there are two types of PPPR: primary and secondary PPPR. Primary PPPR means that an article that has been published before the traditional peer-review process (single- or double-blind) and is open for comments and reviews by peers. Primary PPPR has not been taken up by journals and publishers, but it can be argued that it has been widely accepted as a form of peer review on preprint servers. Secondary PPPR means that an article is open for comments and reviews only after it has been published and after the peer-review process. In addition to the publication platform, secondary PPPR can be conducted on third-party platforms, including PubPeer (https://pubpeer.com) and online journal clubs hosted on general social media sites. F1000 Research is one of the earliest and most discussed platforms for (secondary) PPPR.

It should be noted that, however, PPPR has existed long before publications, peer reviews and comments could be posted online. Letters to editors, commentaries and book reviews are the longest-standing forms of PPPR. They have also been regarded as important forms of scholarly communication and post-publication peer review. However, these traditional forms of PPPR are not without disadvantages: first, the publication decision is in the hands of the editor(s); second, there are limitations in length and the number of references; and third, the responses are often delayed, depending on the publication frequency of a journal (O'Sullivan, Ma and Doran, 2021).

Peer review and scholarly communication

Peer-reviewed publications are given authority and trustworthiness. In research evaluation, publications in peer-reviewed journals are regarded as more important than invited contributions. In university teaching, students are asked to use peer-reviewed materials in their assignments and writings. In mass media and public discourse, peer-reviewed materials are given a stamp of authority with the assumption that facts are substantiated and claims have been justified. In the course of scholarly communication, peer review performs the function of vetting research and legitimising claims and findings. It is the most trusted process that upholds scholarly values and norms; and the rigour of the peer-review process has earned research institutions and researchers public trust. Peer review is also a process by which research integrity is maintained. Traditional or open, peer review is one important form of scholarly communication, ensuring that research outputs and publications contribute to scholarly discourse, scientific progress and public good. Essentially, peer review is a form of scholarly communication in and of itself. Traditional peer review, single- or double-blind, facilitates discussions between authors and reviewers and is mediated by editors. Open peer review and post-publication peer review encourage more participants to engage and interact. From an author's perspective, the peer-review process is an important consideration when choosing where to publish, especially when timing is crucial and when biases and conservatism may be an issue.

6
Research Metrics

Introduction

The number of publications has been used as a form of recognition in scientific research since the late 19th century, concurrent with the development of scientific publishing (Csiszar, 2018). In many disciplines, the number of publications is an important indicator of researchers' productivity and performance; they are sometimes used as a proxy in research assessment involved in the process of recruitment, tenure and promotion and grant applications. The phrase 'publish or perish' has been used to describe the significance of publications in research culture. Eugene Garfield's invention of the Journal Impact Factor (JIF) creates another 'measure' in research evaluation: citations. The rationale is that the more an article is cited, the more impactful it is. Citation-based metrics are then used to assess the quality of research in the STEM disciplines and are currently used in tools for benchmarking and tracking research performance of individuals, research groups and institutions. In this chapter, the term 'research metrics' refers to metrics generally used in research evaluation, including the number of publications and citations, as well as citation-based metrics and indicators.

Citation indexes were first conceptualised and invented as a bibliographic tool for facilitating information access and retrieval. In his seminal paper, Eugene Garfield envisions 'a bibliographic system for science literature that can eliminate the uncritical citation of fraudulent, incomplete, or obsolete data by making it possible for the conscientious scholar to be aware of criticisms of earlier papers' (Garfield, 1955, 108). Garfield founded the Institute for Scientific Information (ISI) and created the Science Citation Index (SCI). In 1972, he published the article, 'Citation Analysis as a Tool in Journal Evaluation' (Garfield, 1972), which illustrates the use of citation counts to assist collection development. Over time, publications in high-impact journals become perceived as more significant and the JIF is used not only for evaluating journals, but also individuals, notwithstanding that the JIF is a journal-level metric.

Today, citation-based metrics are often used as indicators of research quality and impact. These metrics, however, are based on different data sources and methods and many are not appropriate for evaluating individuals' research performance. Hence, these differences must be understood when used in journal evaluation and research assessments. This chapter provides an overview of the functions and uses of some commonly used indicators, in four categories: journal-level metrics, article-level metrics, composite metrics and altmetrics, followed by some considerations of data providers and coverage and a discussion of the responsible metrics movement.

Journal-level metrics

Journal-level metrics are used to represent the impact of a journal – not individual articles or individual researchers – based on citation counts. Amongst them all, the JIF is the most widely known and has been regarded as the gold standard in many disciplines. High-impact journals, for instance, usually refer to journals with a high JIF, with alternatives such as CiteScore and Source Normalised Impact Per Paper (SNIP). Journal-level metrics are primarily based on citation counts, but there are differences in (1) the number of years in the calculation, (2) whether the indicator is normalised and (3) whether the citations are weighted.

Journal impact factor (JIF)

The journal impact factor, or impact factor, is generated and provided by Clarivate's Web of Science (Clarivate, n.d.-a). JIF is calculated based on the ratio of a journal's received citations divided by the number of citable items in a two-year period:

> Citations in 2021 to items published in 2019 + 2020 / Number of citable items in 2019 + 2020

In calculating JIF, citable items include articles and reviews, but do not include editorials, letters and news items. The two-year window is based on the evidence that articles reach a citation peak after two years in many research fields. The WoS provides a five-year journal impact factor for research areas that reach citation peaks over longer periods of time.

The citations are sourced from the collections indexed on WoS, including:

- Science Citation Index
- Social Science Citation Index
- Arts & Humanities Citation Index

- Proceedings Citation Index
- Book Citation Index
- Emerging Sources Citation Index

It should be noted that citations from sources not indexed on WoS will not be counted towards JIF. This is one of the reasons that citation counts can be different on WoS, Scopus, Google Scholar and other data providers. The coverage of the three indexes will be discussed later in this chapter.

CiteScore

CiteScore, provided by Scopus (Scopus, n.d.-a), is based on the number of citations to documents by a journal over four years, divided by the number of the same document types in that journal in the same four years. Documents can include articles, reviews, conference papers, book chapters and data papers.

For example, the CiteScore of the journal *The Lancet* in 2000 was 91.5, calculated based on:

147,190 citations to documents in *The Lancet* 2017–2020 / 1,609 documents in *The Lancet* 2017–2020

CiteScore only counts the citations from documents indexed on Scopus and every citation is counted equally (not weighted). It means that if your article is cited in e.g. *Libellarium*, a journal published in Croatia that is not indexed on Scopus, then the citation will not be counted in CiteScore and other metrics provided on the platform.

The four-year window is considered more appropriate for disciplines where the frequency of publications is less than those in the applied sciences and engineering. For example, articles published in a sociology journal typically take longer to be read and cited. Hence, a four-year window is more realistic for representing the citation impact. In reality, some articles have a longer shelf life and may take longer to accumulate citations, especially those in the humanistic social sciences.

SCImago journal rank (SJR)

SCImago journal rank (SJR) is based on weighted citations by a journal. The weighting is determined by the prestige of a journal, considering the subject field, quality and reputation. A journal must also be indexed by Scopus to be considered as prestigious. In calculating SJR, a citation from a source with a high SJR is worth more than a citation from a source with a lower SJR. In other words, citations from prestigious journals have a positive impact on SJR, whereas citations from lower-ranked journals do not necessarily improve a journal's SJR.

Source normalised impact per paper (SNIP)

Source normalised impact per paper (SNIP) measures actual citations received relative to citations expected in the journal's subject field:

> Number of citations received / Citation potential

The citation potential represents the likelihood of being cited in a particular field and is based on the average number of references per document citing the journal.

SNIP aims to resolve inappropriate comparison due to disciplinary differences and citing practices by calculating impact based on citation potential in a research area. For example, JIF and CiteScores can give the wrong perception that a journal in public health is 'better' than a journal in history based on citation counts. SNIP provides a more balanced view by comparing journals within the same subject area.

Why consider journal-level metrics?

Journals of higher journal-level metrics are more likely to be read and cited. They can reach a wider audience internationally, since they are usually prioritised and subscribed to by academic libraries. Journals not indexed on WoS do not have a JIF; likewise, journals not indexed on Scopus do not have a CiteScore. Therefore, there is a certain level of credibility and reputation associated with journal-level metrics: indexed journals meet the selection criteria for quality control. Journal-level metrics can provide some insights into the visibility, quality and impact of journals and they are widely used in research evaluation at individual and institutional levels. When choosing where to publish, a researcher is naturally opting for good-quality and high-impact journals that 'count' in research assessments. However, journal-level metrics should not be treated as proxies for quality and impact, since they can be affected by various factors:

1 **Disciplinary differences:** Publication and citing practices vary in different disciplines. Citation counts are considered less, if at all, important in disciplines in pure and theoretical sciences and the arts and humanities. Unlike the applied sciences, researchers do not necessarily develop a study or build an argument based on the most recent

experiments or research findings; rather, their work can be in dialogues with materials published long ago or the recent past. Their work also tends to include fewer citations. Moreover, when journal articles and other research outputs are cited in monographs, they are often not counted because the coverage of monographs is limited on WoS and Scopus. It is important to note that although citation counts are useful to estimate the quality and impact of journals in some disciplines, they can be misleading in others.

2 **General and specialised journals:** In most disciplines, some journals cover a wider range of topics, while others focus on more specialised research areas. Journals of general interests tend to have higher citation counts as they appeal to a wider audience than specialised journals. However, a lower journal-level metric does not mean that a journal is of less importance for an author. In fact, an article in a specialised journal can make substantial contributions by engaging the right audience. Hence, journal-level metrics should be interpreted by taking into account the size of the research community in the subject area and, more importantly, the target audience of an article.

3 **Languages:** The majority of journals indexed on WoS and Scopus are in English, meaning that the citation counts by most non-English language journals are not counted. At the same time, the journal-level metrics of non-English language journals are not available because they are not indexed on WoS or Scopus. Similar to specialised journals, non-English-language journals are tailored for readers and researchers in specific regions and their importance and contributions cannot be solely determined by journal-level metrics.

Most importantly, journal-level metrics are indicators of the quality and impact of *journals*. It is inappropriate to use them for evaluating individual articles or individual researchers. When using journal-level metrics, it is necessary to take into consideration disciplinary differences and citing practices, as well as specialisms, languages and target audience of a journal. Journal-level metrics are not suitable for evaluating the research performance of individual researchers.

Article-level metrics

The field-weighted citation impact (FWCI), provided by Scopus, is the key citation-based metric at the article level. FWCI is often used for benchmarking and ranking research performance between research groups, departments, universities and countries. Other article-level metrics include the raw number of citations, downloads, views and so on. These metrics are useful for tracking the engagement and reach of an article. It should also be noted that an article with a high article-level metric can be published in a journal of high or low journal-level metric.

Field-weighted citation impact (FWCI)

Field-weighted citation impact (FWIC) is the ratio of the total citations received by an article (or research output) and the total number of citations expected based on the average of the subject field:

- A FWCI of exactly 1 means that the article (or research output) performs as expected at the average level.
- A FWCI of more than 1 means that the article (or research output) is cited more than expected compared to the average. For example, an article of a FWCI 1.35 means that it is 35% more cited than expected.
- A FWCI of less than 1 means that an article is cited less than expected compared to the global average.

FWCI is useful in gauging the research impact of an article by comparing the number of citations received and the average in a subject area. It is a more appropriate indicator than journal-level metrics when it comes to an article or a group of research outputs or researchers. To a certain extent, the indicator is normalised within a subject category. However, the general limitations of citation-based metrics apply. FWCI may not be indicative when basic and applied research are lumped into the same subject category. For example, works in theoretical physics tend to receive substantially fewer citations than those in applied physics; as such, a theoretical physicist tends to have an FWCI below 1 if basic and applied physics research are counted in the same category.

Number of views, downloads and citations

Many publishing platforms provide the number of views, downloads and citations of an article. Views and downloads are usually 'raw' numbers in the sense that they are counted as long as someone visited a web page or downloaded an article. These counts are not seen as important as citation-based metrics, because it can be argued that potential readers may browse or download an article without reading and there can also be multiple views and downloads by the same person. Nevertheless, the number of views and downloads can be used to demonstrate the reach and impact of an article; they can be particularly helpful in research areas where the number of citations is less relevant.

The raw citation counts of an article can be found on some journal websites, Scopus, WoS, Google Scholar, Crossref (Crossref, n.d.) and other services. These counts can be different due to the coverage of the data providers and indexes. They are the basis on which many citation-based metrics are calculated. From an author's perspective, it is most useful when the counts are linked to the citing articles, that is, the authors can trace where and how their works have been cited.

Altmetric
Altmetric is used to demonstrate the attention and influence of research on a variety of platforms and documents, including public policy documents, research blogs, mainstream media coverage, bookmarks on reference managers such as Mendeley and mentions on social networks (www.altmetric.com). Compared with traditional publication- and citation-based metrics, altmetrics are useful for demonstrating research impact beyond research communities and they can be incorporated into research profiles. Similar to the number of downloads and views, they can be used as alternatives in gauging the reach and influence of an article.

Altmetric collects and analyses data by tracking research identifiers, including PubMedID, arXivID, ADS ID, SSRN ID, RePEC ID, Handle.net identifiers, URN identifiers, ISBNs and DOIs; nevertheless, the data sources and collection are less stable than traditional citation-based metrics. There are also concerns about gaming (e.g. Twitter bots) and missing data, e.g. citations in policy documents are not easily captured. Generally speaking, altmetric is not considered as important as publication- and citation-based metrics in research evaluation, but it is increasingly used to indicate societal and policy impacts.

Composite metrics: h-index
H-index is a composite indicator invented by Jorge Hirsch (Hirsch, 2005). The indicator is used to demonstrate the performance of an individual based on both the number of published articles and the number of citations, representing productivity and impact. The h-index is required in some funding applications and it is used in the methodology of QS subject rankings (Lane, 2023). However, the h-index can overestimate or underestimate the performance or productivity of a researcher. For example, if a researcher is listed as one of the authors in many publications of their research team, then their h-index can be very high even though they were only responsible for a small part of the study. It is because the h-index does not differentiate between their and their colleagues' contributions. As a result, their h-index

can be as high as others who may have contributed more substantially. Contrarily, a researcher, say, a philosopher, who published a magnum opus that has been discussed and reviewed widely and has accumulated over ten thousand citations over time. Yet, their h-index will stay as one despite the book's considerable influences. Studies have shown that the h-index can be inconsistent (e.g. Waltman and van Eck, 2012) and caution its inappropriate uses in research evaluation. For instance, ranking grant or job applications by h-index is an unintelligible and ill-considered exercise.

Data providers and coverage

Since most metrics are based on publication and citation counts, they can be affected by the coverage and collection policy of the data providers. A researcher may ask: 'Why do I have different metrics on Google Scholar and Scopus? Which one can I trust or include in my research profile? Are these metrics standardised measures?' These questions can be answered by comparing the three most discussed services: Google Scholar, Scopus and WoS.

Google Scholar

Google Scholar is a free service on the world wide web. Similar to the search engine Google, it searches and indexes scholarly publications using its web crawler with links to the citing articles. Google Scholar displays the citation counts of each article and lists the total number of citations and h-index on researchers' profiles. Google Scholar does not have a collection policy or specific selection criteria other than the algorithmic identification of scholarly publications. Hence, it has a wider coverage than Scopus and Web of Science, including more books and book chapters as well as non-English language publications.

The wider coverage is beneficial for researchers to trace and track citations from publications not indexed on Scopus and Web of Science, especially journals published in non-English-speaking countries. These citations can better indicate the research impact in a global context. Although there are potential issues of duplication of publications and citations, there have been fewer instances due to the use of Digital Object Identifiers (DOIs) and research profiles on ORCID (https://orcid.org).

However, a concerning issue is the inclusion of predatory journals (see Chapter 2), especially those that engage in gaming strategies with artificially high citation counts. If citation counts and h-index on Google Scholar are to be used for research evaluation and other research purposes, it is crucial to check and review the sources of citations.

Scopus

Established in 2004, Scopus is a product of the publisher Elsevier. It provides indexing services and bibliometric data including citation counts, citation ranks, CiteScore, SJR and SNIP. Users can also view trends of specific journals and profiles of individual researchers. Scopus is a subscription service and is not freely available. It is widely used by academic libraries and research data analytics services. The datasets are also used in research products, university rankings and national research assessment exercises. SciVal, an affiliated product based on Scopus data, is widely used by research managers and administrators to benchmark performances of individuals, groups and institutions.

In terms of coverage, Scopus is more comprehensive than WoS, particularly in the social sciences and humanities, but it is less extensive than Google Scholar. It has a collection and indexing policy (Scopus, n.d.-b) to ensure the quality of the journals indexed. However, its practice has been criticised for its Anglo-American biases (Mills et al., 2021) because most indexed journals are in English. Local studies, particularly those published by learned societies rather than commercial publishers (for example, *Journal of Irish Archaeology*) are not indexed.

Web of Science (WoS)

Web of Science (Wos) was developed as a product of Eugene Garfield's Institute for Scientific Information. The indexing service has been regarded as the authoritative source of high-impact journals globally, especially in STEM disciplines. Their coverage in the social sciences and humanities is less comprehensive in comparison to Scopus and Google Scholar. WoS is a major data source for bibliometric and scientometric research. It has also been used as the data source for national research assessment exercises such as the Research Excellence Framework, commonly known as the UK REF.

The WoS core collection does not boast a wide and comprehensive coverage; rather, the collection is curated based on 24 quality criteria (Clarivate, n.d.-b). The initial steps involve reviewing basic information including ISSN, journal URL, journal publishers, presence of peer-review policy, followed by the examination of scholarly contents, presence of ethics statements, editorial and author affiliation details. After the screening stage, the quality and impact of journals are important criteria for inclusion in the WoS collections, including citation analysis of authors and editorial board members. The set criteria are useful for validating the quality and impact of journals; however, they can be exclusive for the arts and humanities, non-English-language journals, as well as journals in new and emerging research areas, due to a lack of citation track record.

Matthew effect

The Matthew effect is often discussed in the context of research metrics. The basic idea can be described as 'the rich get richer': when a journal has established a track record, it is more likely that it will continue to attract more attention and citations. Thus, an established journal has a cumulative advantage over time. The Matthew effect also applies to the track record of researchers. Merton, who coined the term, states that:

> the Matthew effect consists of the accruing of greater increments of recognition for particularly scientific contributions to scientists of considerable repute and the withholding of such recognition from scientists who have not yet made their mark.
>
> (Merton, 1973, 446)

Although it is unlikely that the Matthew effect can be eradicated, it should be noted in the evaluation of new and emerging journals, as well as early-career researchers, especially those from less privileged backgrounds. Ma (2022) has argued that the very use of research metrics is a cause of epistemic injustice because works of peripheral groups are systematically marginalised. Put another way, their works are not visible due to the Matthew effect enhanced by rankings of journals and articles on WoS, Scopus and Google Scholar.

Responsible metrics

Research metrics are useful in many ways. Authors and institutions can use them to monitor and track the reach and impact of research articles and scholarly journals. Metrics can also be analysed by researchers in bibliometrics and scientometrics to understand the networks of scholarly communication and scientific progress. However, when research metrics are used as proxies in research evaluation, they become a goal rather than a measure (commonly known as Goodhart's Law). Studies have shown that the use of metrics in research evaluation has led to cultural change in knowledge production and scholarly communication including gaming behaviour (de Rijcke et al., 2016) and even misconduct and manipulation in academic research (Biagioli and Lippman, 2020). There are also concerns about the decline of 'bibliodiversity', in the sense that publications in some subject areas can be marginalised due to their low citation impact. These concerns have led to the discussion and advocacy of *responsible metrics* and research assessment reforms. The most commonly known declarations are *DORA*, *The Leiden Manifesto*, *The Hong Kong Principles* and *The Metric Tide Report* and most recently, the *Agreement on Reforming Research Assessment*.

DORA

DORA is the acronym for the San Francisco Declaration of Research Assessment (https://sfdora.org). The Declaration was developed during a meeting of the American Society for Cell Biology in San Francisco, California, in 2012. The key issues are the overemphasis of journal impact factor (JIF) in research evaluation and the necessity of recognition and rewards for research outputs such as dataset, code, software and patent. Individual researchers, research institutions, universities, funders and publishers can become a signatory of DORA. DORA also organises workshops and compiles case studies, resources and toolkits for those interested in responsible research assessments.

The Leiden Manifesto

Named after a conference held in Leiden in 2014, the Leiden Manifesto recommends best practices for metrics-based research assessment. The ten principles (Hicks et al., 2015) respond to the widespread 'abuse of research metrics' in research evaluation:

1 Quantitative evaluation should support qualitative, expert assessment.
2 Measure performance against the research missions of the institution, group or researcher.
3 Protect excellence in locally relevant research.
4 Keep data collection and analytical processes open, transparent and simple.
5 Allow those evaluated to verify data and analysis.
6 Account for variation by field in publication and citation practices.
7 Base assessment of individual researchers on a qualitative judgement of their portfolio.
8 Avoid misplaced concreteness and false precision.
9 Recognise the systemic effects of assessment and indicators.
10 Scrutinise indicators regularly and update them.

The Hong Kong Manifesto

This was developed as part of the 6th World Conference on Research Integrity held in Hong Kong, with emphasis on 'robust, rigorous and transparent practices' in evidence-based assessments of researchers (Moher et al., 2020). There is a strong emphasis on the strengthening of research integrity and the principles include:

1 Assess researchers on responsible practices from conception to delivery, including the development of research idea, research design, methodology, execution and effective dissemination.
2 Value the accurate and transparent reporting of all research, regardless of the results.
3 Value the practices of open science (open research) – such as open methods, materials and data.
4 Value a broad range of research and scholarship, such as replication, innovation, translation, synthesis and meta-research.
5 Value a range of other contributions to responsible research and scholarly activity, such as peer review for grants and publications, mentoring, outreach and knowledge exchange.

The rationale and current implementation (examples) of these principles are provided in the manifesto.

The Metric Tide Report

This is an independent review of the uses of metrics in research assessment and management in the UK and internationally. The findings show that the understanding of metrics is contested and open to misunderstandings, while inappropriate indicators create perverse incentives. The report proposes:

> the notion of *responsible metrics* as a way of framing appropriate uses of quantitative indicators in the governance, management and assessment of research with the following dimensions:
>
> 1 Robustness: basing metrics on the best possible data in terms of accuracy and scope
> 2 Humility: recognising that quantitative evaluation should support – but not supplant – qualitative, expert assessment
> 3 Transparency: keeping data collection and analytical processes open and transparent, so that those being evaluated can test and verify the results
> 4 Diversity: accounting for variation by field and using a variety of indicators to support diversity across the research system
> 5 Reflexivity: recognising systemic and potential effects of indicators and updating them in response.
>
> (Wilsdon et al., 2015)

In addition, the report also identifies 20 recommendations for: (a) supporting the effective leadership, governance and management of research cultures; (b) improving the data infrastructure that supports research information management; (c) increasing the usefulness of existing data and information sources; and (d) co-ordinating activity and building evidence.

The Coalition for Advancing Research Assessment

The Coalition (https://coara.eu) was initiated in 2022 during the drafting of the Agreement on reforming research assessment, involving 350 organisations from over 40 countries. The signatories include major funding agencies, universities and learned societies and associations. The ten commitments of the Agreement (CoARA, 2022) include:

1. Recognise the diversity of contributions to and careers in, research in accordance with the needs and nature of the research.
2. Base research assessment primarily on qualitative evaluation for which peer review is central, supported by responsible use of quantitative indicators.
3. Abandon inappropriate uses in research of journal- and publication-based metrics, in particular inappropriate uses of journal impact factor (JIF) and h-index.
4. Avoid the use of rankings of research organisations in research assessment.
5. Commit resources to reforming research assessment as is needed to achieve the organisational changes committed to.
6. Review and develop research assessment criteria, tools and processes.
7. Raise awareness of research assessment reform and provide transparent communication, guidance and training on assessment criteria and processes as well as their use.
8. Exchange practices and experiences to enable mutual learning within and beyond the Coalition.
9. Communicate progress made and adherence to the Principles and implementation of the Commitments.
10. Evaluate practices, criteria and tools based on solid evidence and the state of the art in research on research and make data openly available for evidence gathering and research.

Research metrics and scholarly communication

When one is choosing where to publish, research metrics are indicative of the quality and impact of a journal. Publishing in a journal with a good track record is beneficial for reaching a wider audience. In some disciplines, they are considered important in a research career. Nevertheless, citation-based metrics are not and should not be the only factor. At times it is more fruitful to address and engage the research community in a specialised journal, not to mention that research metrics are irrelevant in some research domains. Nevertheless, as research metrics remain significant in research assessment, it is essential to distinguish the different types of research metrics: journal-level metrics are not suitable for evaluating individuals or articles, whilst article-level metrics can be used when disciplinary norms are thoughtfully considered. A clear understanding of what an indicator represents and how it is calculated is essential for appropriate uses and interpretation.

Studies have shown that the overemphasis and misuses of research metrics induce a hypercompetitive research culture (de Rijcke et al., 2016; Wellcome Trust, 2020), which in turn leads to gaming practices in research and publication and concerns about research integrity (Biagioli and Lippman, 2020). The uses of research metrics are also in tension with the open access movement, due to the very fact that researchers are discouraged from supporting new diamond open access journals when they do not have a track record of metrics and are not yet indexed on WoS and Scopus. Scholarly communication librarians are tasked with publicising the appropriate and inappropriate uses of research metrics and their limitations. For instance, many are engaged in developing the statement of responsible metrics in their universities and involved in the conversations about research assessment reform.

Online resources
- **The Bibliomagician** Comment and practical guidance from the LIS-Bibliometrics community. https://thebibliomagician.wordpress.com
- **Competency Model for Bibliometric Work** The competency model can help to identify skills gaps, support progression through career stages and to prepare job descriptions in the field of bibliometrics. https://thebibliomagician.wordpress.com/competencies.
- **DORA Resource Library** A collection of materials to facilitate the development of responsible research and researcher assessment policies and practices. https://sfdora.org/resource-library.
- **Metrics Toolkit** The Metrics Toolkit provides evidence-based information about research metrics across disciplines, including how each metric is calculated, where you can find it and how each should (and should not) be applied. www.metrics-toolkit.org/metrics.
- **Research Impact Things** A self-paced training programme about research impact. https://iatulimpactthings.info.
- **Responsible metrics** Evidence and advocacy for responsible research assessment. https://responsiblemetrics.org.

7
Societal Impact

Introduction

Societal impact is a broad term that describes the impact of research *outside academia*, defined as 'an effect on, change or benefit to the economy, society, culture, public policy or services, health, the environment or quality of life, beyond academia' in the UK REF (Research Excellence Framework) 2014 (UKRI, 2022). This definition includes cultural, economic, educational, environmental, health, political, social and technological impacts and has been adapted by funding agencies and research institutions. An important element in the understanding of societal impact is *change*: how does research bring changes to human and social behaviour, professional practices, public policies, health and environmental conditions, welfare and wellbeing and our understanding of cultures, societies and nature.

The original Logic Model Development Guide was published by the Kellogg Foundation (2004) for tracing the policy influences on development and planning and it has been adapted to conceptualise the societal impact of research. The logic model (also known as 'linear model') describes the pathway progressing from inputs and research activities, to research outputs (e.g. publications), outcomes and impacts (Penfield et al., 2014). It is a useful visualisation for researchers to envision societal impacts, including the five stages (Figure 7.1):

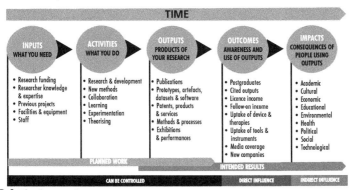

Figure 7.1 *The impact journey*

In reality, however, impact pathways are usually not linear and are dependent on many factors. Based on an analysis of impact case studies collected in 16 European countries, Muhonen, Benneworth and Olmos-Peñuela (2020) developed a typology of 12 impact pathways in four major categories, indicating that impacts can be planned (e.g. anticipation of anniversaries) but can also be accidental (e.g. the development of vaccines for a new disease):

1 *Dissemination* includes the interactive dissemination pathway, where key stakeholders become aware of research findings disseminated through publications, social media, mass media and so on.
2 *Cocreation* includes the collaboration pathway, the public engagement pathway, the expertise pathway and the mobility pathway. These pathways involve working with key stakeholders in creating societal impacts.
3 *Reacting to societal change* includes the 'anticipating anniversaries pathway', the 'seize the day' pathway, the social innovation pathway and the commercialisation pathway. These pathways illustrate the ways by which research responds to anticipated and unanticipated events, as well as business opportunities.
4 *Driving societal change* includes the 'research engagement as a key to impact' pathway, the knowledge 'creeps' into society pathway and the building 'new epistemic communities' pathway. These pathways show the diffusion of knowledge with both tangible and intangible impacts.

These different pathways demonstrate the many ways by which a research project can create and achieve societal impact. In other words, the impact journey is not necessarily a linear progression: sometimes societal impact is brought by natural disasters or crises, whilst at other times they can be anticipated. Achieving societal impact often involves working closely with community members or business partners; some also engage in public discussions and debates on traditional mass media, social media and other platforms. Societal impact activities require interactions with stakeholders in different sectors of society.

Planning for societal impact

Researchers are increasingly encouraged and motivated to demonstrate the societal impact of their research projects. It is pertinent to understand how a research project can change the ways we understand nature and culture and the ways we live and work; or whether a research project can lead to innovative technologies and create job opportunities; or what contributions a research project can make in shaping civic debates and public policies. The demonstration of societal impact can invite support from businesses, governments and civic organisations, while accounting for public funds and resources at institutional level. Researchers can also include societal impact in their research portfolios.

Whether a researcher is planning to write an impact statement for a grant application or an impact case study in the future, societal impacts can be abstract and vague. What are the potential or actual societal impacts of a research project? How can they be articulated? Is it possible to plan societal impact? Essentially, societal impact is collaborative and cumulative; it can also be unexpected and difficult to anticipate. As a result, it may seem a daunting task when a researcher has to come up with a narrative of extraordinary impacts that may sound like exaggerations or even mere fiction. In reality, many researchers are making 'normal' impacts in their everyday research activities and interactions with businesses, organisations and the general public. They only need a plan to record and track their activities 'related to dedicated activities following strategic choices and objectives' (Sivertsen and Meijer, 2020, 67). Incorporating impact activities in a research plan or project can enhance the visibility and publicity of research, which can then be used as evidence of impact.

Impact activities are designed to engage with people and organisations outside academia: school children, vulnerable communities, businesses, journalists, government departments, politicians and so on. Before reaching out and planning activities, researchers should consider the feasibility of impact activities including such factors as resources, networks and organisational support. The following prompts can be used to reflect on the research plan or project:

Who will benefit from your research in the short, medium and long term?
When brainstorming societal impact goals and activities, it is useful to envision how a research project contributes to societal impacts in the short and long term. Some research projects are designed with societal challenges in mind and their long-term societal impacts tend to be easier to articulate: whether it is to reduce inequalities or to protect marine life, they will contribute to tangible and observable changes. Although it may seem difficult to evidence long-term impacts of a project, it is not impossible to document the ways by which a research project's normal contributions that can lead to incremental changes. These can include publication of non-academic research outputs such as blogs, white papers and policy briefs, as well as citations and adaptations in community and professional practices.

Some research projects aim to understand culture and history for a better understanding of humanity and society, while others ponder and explore unknown dimensions and relationships in thoughts and nature. The long-term societal impacts are often untraceable in observable ways or measurable terms since the creation of societal impacts is mainly through the diffusion of knowledge in higher education. Nevertheless, researchers can contribute by engaging and educating the public utilising non-traditional research outputs such as podcasts and exhibitions (see Chapter 2).

Here are a few brainstorming questions that can help with envisioning the long- and short-term societal impacts:

- Will your research inform public discussions of societal and global challenges?
- Will your research project potentially lead to changes in community or professional practices or innovative approaches?
- Will your research project potentially lead to changes in policy?
- Will your research project potentially lead to improvements in health and wellbeing?
- Will your research project potentially build capacity for a new industry?

Why is it important that the beneficiaries are informed by your research?
Once you have a vision (or some ideas) of how your research can contribute to societal impacts, it is then useful to ask *who* should be informed about your research and why. When we explain why it is important for an audience to know about something, it is also asking if they can be the potential beneficiaries of an impact activity. After all, if there is not a good reason for a group of people to be informed, then it is less likely that they will benefit from your research and there will be no societal impacts! Does your research project speak directly to practitioners, policymakers or the general public? Articulating the reasons why they would want to know more from your research project can clarify the scope and objectives of an impact activity.

In other words, the planning of impact activities becomes more realistic when your target audience has reasons to know more about your research. For example, why would the general public like to know about a renewed interpretation of the origins of The Great War? Or, why would policymakers be interested in the findings of (un)ethical practices of machine learning in artificial intelligence research? While your vision of societal impacts is long-term, the planning of impact activities should focus on those who can benefit from your impact activities and non-academic publications. It is more likely that they will share what they've learned from the impact activity with more people and make use of the new knowledge in schools, businesses and communities, which may in turn influence professional practices, new products, or policymaking.

What kinds of publications and activities will engage and interest your target audience?
Now you have a vision of societal impacts of your research and you have identified the target audience, it is time to consider how to engage with them. Impact activities can involve public engagement and outreach, non-academic publications and relationship building with stakeholders. Some activities demand significant time and resources, while others are less resource-intensive. There is not a one-size-fits-all model. It is all about communicating your research, whether it is to spark curiosity, to foster innovation or to inform policy.

Public engagement and outreach activities can include public talks, school visits and exhibitions, as well as podcasts, videos and social media posts. These activities are designed to engage the target audience directly, while their impacts can be amplified by media attention and coverage. The long-term impacts of these activities can be difficult to measure, but it is possible to track the number of visitors, listeners or viewers on websites and social media platforms. Yet it is important to bear in mind that these metrics and indicators are not comparable and should be interpreted *in situ*, as different impact activities are tailored for different audiences in different locales.

Non-academic publications include white papers, reports and policy briefs. These publications often include research questions and research findings, but they assume no prior knowledge of the subject matter and they avoid the use of jargon or specialist terms where possible because they aim to inform non-academic or non-specialist audiences. In some research institutions, these non-academic publications count towards research outputs. They are effective means to present evidence for policymakers and politicians and they can also inform the public about latest developments and findings. The number of views and downloads can be documented. It is possible for citations in policy documents to be tracked by products such as Altmetric and overton.io.

Other non-academic research outputs include personal and professional blogs, news platforms and podcasts and videos. Blogs are a genre that has been successful in engaging academic and non-academic audiences in the discussion of research results as well as ongoing topics of interest. Similarly, researchers are encouraged to 'translate' their research for publication in digital newspapers and magazines. These blogs and news articles are good venues to illustrate why a research topic is interesting and important.

Similarly, podcasts and videos have become popular media. Many universities host public lecture series on YouTube, while there are podcasts produced by historians, linguists, philosophers and scientists.

All kinds of impact activities involve building relationships with non-academic collaborators such as businesses, community partners, cultural and non-profit organisations, government departments and policymakers. These activities are building blocks for longer-term impacts in society.

Research for policy

Research for policy has been advocated by national and supranational agencies such as the European Commission in recent years, with the mission to increase and enhance the use of research in policy making. Research for policy can create societal impact as the process informs the public and politicians and stimulates civic and political debates. Global challenges such as climate crisis and pandemics often require expert knowledge in different domains of knowledge; that is to say, tackling these challenges not only require technical and technological solutions but also the understanding of human behaviour and economic and social impacts. For one, historical knowledge can shed light on risks and mishaps in the past in times of crisis and unrest, while artistic performances, exhibitions and storytelling can be more powerful than hard facts when it comes to policy implementation.

The institutional structure of research for policy is in development in many countries. It is because when researchers are prompted to create societal impact, they have no available channels where they can advise or suggest relevant expert knowledge. Likewise, policymakers are at a loss when expert knowledge is required for the development or drafting of policy. There is a clear need for a platform where subject expertise and policy needs can meet. In addition, both researchers and policymakers face challenges when communicating with each other.

Research for policy requires a set of skills for communicating research effectively. Don't researchers share and discuss their findings on a regular basis? They do – however, they are communicating with their peers and most are in their research area, meaning that they tend to elaborate on the minute details in methodology and converse in terminologies and jargon. These materials are likely to be illegible and irrelevant in a policymaking setting. It is also common for researchers to speak with uncertainties. The very nature of research is that there can always be new discoveries and questions – however, uncertainties are not the best science advice for policymaking!

To enhance policy impact, it is necessary for researchers to better understand science communication in policy context. The European Commission Joint Research Committee (JRC) has developed a comprehensive competence framework for researchers, which includes five key areas: understanding policy, participate in policy making, communicate, engage with citizens and stakeholders, and collaborate. Each addresses knowledge and skills that help understand the specific needs of policymaking, while some are also useful for science communication and public engagement. Table 7.1 illustrates the competences required under each key area or 'competence cluster'.

Table 7.1 Competence framework 'Science for Policy' for researchers (European Commission, 2023)

Understanding policy	Participate in policymaking	Communicate	Engage with citizens and stakeholders	Collaborate
Evidence needs	Knowledge brokering	Community mindset	Engagement mindset	Collaborative mindset
Policy relationships and networks	Working with values	Clear writing	Planning and designing citizen engagement	Group dynamics
Monitoring and evaluation of impact	Political sensitivity	Speaking with impact	Planning and designing stakeholder consultation	Empathy and emotion
	Drafting briefings	Storytelling and visual literacy		Intercultural sensitivity
	Writing for policymakers	Dealing with mis and disinformation		Systems thinking
	Communities of practices and networks	Interacting with different media		Convening and facilitating
		Communicating scientific uncertainty		

Research for policy is an important aspect of societal impact and can make immediate impact with long-term significance. It is an area of importance for meeting the United Nations Sustainable Development Goals (SDGs) and global, national and local challenges from climate crisis to the preservation of cultural heritage.

Ex ante and ex post impact assessments

Societal impact is sometimes formally assessed. *Ex ante* impact assessment means that the evaluation is based on societal impact not yet realised but expected in the impact statement (or 'pathways to impact') in a grant application. *Ex post* impact assessment means that the evaluation is based on actual and realised societal impact in an impact case study. In the UK REF, *ex post* impact assessment is an important component that can affect the allocation of block grants to public universities.

Impact statements for grant applications

Many funding programmes require an impact statement (or 'pathway to impact') in grant applications. Researchers are expected to articulate the potential societal impacts of the proposed research project: What changes will it make? Why is it important to tackle these problems and issues? How is it beneficial for the economy and industry, local communities and global populations? For some, writing impact statements can be like writing fiction. Researchers are reluctant to predict societal impacts because they cannot be certain that the research project will yield useful results. Studies have shown that peer review of impact statements can be random, inconsistent and biased (European Science Foundation, 2012; NABI, 2018), while others show a preference for short-term commercial impacts (de Jong, Smit and van Drooge, 2016; Ma et al., 2020).

To improve the assessment of impact statements, there are suggestions to focus on process-oriented impacts that are more formative than summative. Specifically, Ma and Agnew (2022) have proposed a framework for impact evaluation in grant applications (Table 7.2 opposite), which emphasises the alignment between funding programme objectives and impact evaluation and identifies the activities and processes that contribute to societal impacts. Focusing on process-oriented impacts also means that researchers can articulate their plans for impact activities that can be evidenced.

Impact case studies

Impact case studies are a method for demonstrating actual and realised societal impacts of research. This method is most commonly known in the UK REF impact assessments (UKRI, n.d.). Researchers can submit impact case studies of eight impact types: cultural, economic, environmental, health, legal, political, societal and technological. The impact case studies method has been adapted in countries such as Finland and Norway. However, it should be noted that the use of impact case studies is not always for assessment purposes; for some research institutions and universities, the impact case studies method has been adapted to enrich research culture by showcasing the societal impacts of research.

Table 7.2 *A framework for impact evaluation in grant applications*

Type of funding programme	Basic 'Blue Sky' research	Societal challenges	Collaboration	Public engagement
Aim of funding programmes	Support basic and curiosity-driven research	Address societal challenges, including SDGs and/or national priorities	Encourage collaboration between academia and industry, NGOs and other stakeholders	Enrich cultural understanding and experience and/or promote science communication
Impact	No	Yes	Yes	Yes
What to assess?	N/A	The societal challenges and national priorities the research project aims to address The beneficiaries, practices, or policies the research project aims to inform, influence, or change	The outputs, expected use-based outcomes of the collaboration Expected experience-based outcomes and impacts can also be included The potential of longer-term collaboration The societal challenges and national priorities the collaboration aims to address	The processes and activities the research project plans to undertake The expected experience-based outcomes of the activities The collaborators and participants of the proposed activities

The UK REF impact case studies template includes the following components:
- *Summary of the impact*: A brief description of the specific impact described in the case study
- *Underpinning research*: An outline of the key research insights or findings that underpinned the impact and details of the research undertaken, including any relevant contextual information about the research area
- *References to the research*: The key outputs of the research including academic publications, white papers and other types of outputs
- *Details of the impact*: A clear explanation of the project's societal impact, including the details of beneficiaries, nature of impact and any evidence or indicators of the impact described
- *Sources to corroborate the impact*: Sources that could corroborate key claims made in the previous section, e.g. reports, reviews and web links in the public domain

Challenges of societal impact assessment

There are concerns about the implications and unintended consequences of the 'impact agenda' (Martin, 2011; Watermeyer, 2016), notwithstanding that researchers are in agreement that research and scholarship should contribute to society. It has been argued that, on the one hand, impact assessment can lead to the perception that research projects of instrumental and utilitarian purposes are more desirable, while seemingly devaluing 'knowledge for the sake of knowledge' in basic and pure research. This is due to the fact that societal impact assessments have a preference for outcomes that can be easily monitored and measured.

On the other hand, the criteria for impact assessment are different to set because societal impacts can be tangible and intangible in the short and long term. While there can be plans for monitoring and tracing impacts for research projects designed to tackle local, regional and global societal challenges, the contributions of basic and theoretical research are more difficult to trace. For example, the contributions to vaccine development and health interventions can be documented by the improvements in mortality and health conditions; however, their potential applications in the sciences or adaptations in arts and cultures such as films and video games are not always traceable.

In other words, the criteria for impact assessment are complicated by the wide and varied types of impact: some impacts can be created and planned, while others cannot be predicted; some impacts can be easily monitored and tracked, while others can be difficult to articulate. The most discussed problems and issues include attribution, the counterfactual argument, knowledge creep, time lag and evidence of societal impacts (European Science Foundation, 2012; Penfield et al., 2014):

- *Attribution*: Societal impacts can be attributed to 'serendipitous findings, good fortune and complex networks interacting and translating knowledge and research… through a complex variety of processes, individuals and organizations' (Penfield et al. 2014). It is hence difficult, if not inappropriate, to attribute societal impacts to a specific individual or research project.
- *The counterfactual argument*: Another aspect of attribution is the counterfactual argument: what would have happened without the intervention or research? Would the observed impacts have occurred anyway? A causal relationship can be difficult to establish between a research project and societal impacts.
- *Knowledge creep*: When research contributes to common knowledge, the 'new data and information becomes accepted and gets absorbed over

time' (Penfield et al., 2014). The researchers and research projects are not necessarily mentioned or cited in policy documents or public debates.
- *Time lag*: The time lag between research and societal impacts varies. A research project in the applied sciences can result in patents and licences for industrial production within a few years, whereas the research findings of basic research may take decades to be translated into applied research. An exhibition curated for a commemoration creates immediate societal impacts compared to the general influences of art and literature.
- *Evidence of societal impacts*: Collecting and collating evidence for societal impacts can be challenging. Research findings contribute to and become common knowledge in many pathways and not every piece of evidence can be traced and documented.

The challenges of societal impact assessment are not barriers to achieving societal impacts, however. Evidence of societal impacts can be easier to monitor, collect and record with some planning rather than as an afterthought.

Social media: research and societal impacts
Social media are important platforms for enhancing research and societal impacts. Many researchers share news about their new publications, their participation and presentation at conferences and events relevant to their academic and professional interests. These social networks can reach a wider audience. The effects are significant when a post is shared by accounts with a substantial number of followers. There are various kinds of platforms for sharing research outputs, including preprints, publications, data, source codes and others. Researchers can get in touch with each other or create groups for discussions. In recent years, many researchers have moved onto general social media platforms and create communities, especially Twitter, Reddit and Discord for their connectedness and functionalities.

Networking and public engagement
Social media platforms enable interactions and networking beyond geographical and institutional boundaries. That is to say, they can facilitate networking with researchers from all over the world. Using social media to exchange ideas can gain insights from different perspectives that overcome cultural, linguistic and sometimes even disciplinary boundaries. It is also beneficial for researchers who cannot and do not want to attend overseas conferences for personal and/or environmental reasons.

Twitter journal clubs are popular for researchers to engage in discussion of new publications. Here's how it works: after a journal club selects a paper, participants log on Twitter at a specific time and the online conversation from people around the globe ensues. Some conversations are mediated by a facilitator and some are open discussions. Since most Twitter accounts are open to the public, the discussion can also be followed up after the meeting time. Twitter journal clubs can be a great way to connect with researchers who work in similar topics and may foster future collaborations (McGinnigle et al., 2017) and they are also considered as platforms for learning and community building (Daneshjou and Adamson, 2020; Stoneman and Hiremath, 2020).

Live tweeting is an effective way to promote an event and a community. Organisers of conferences and events can create a hashtag for participants to tweet about an event. These tweets can not only increase the visibility of researchers and their work, but also enable those who cannot attend to follow the key contributions and discussion points. Live tweeting can also be a good way to fully engage in the presentations and discussions, as it requires full attention! As many conference participants follow the hashtag, live tweeting can be a way to open up dialogues with online participants.

As discussed in Chapter 2, blogs and newsletters allow more in-depth and lengthy commentaries and discussions, similar to letters to editors or communication in an academic journal. Some blogs and newsletters have a mediator, though some have no editorial control and no delays. Blogs and newsletters can be used for community building and even post-publication peer review. The participation is less time-sensitive and does not demand instant and rapid responses on platforms such as Twitter.

Researchers can make use of handles (e.g. @facetpublishing) in their social media posts to signify the intended audience – whether the social media post is intended for an interest group, practitioners or policymakers. The owners of the handles will receive a notification of mentions and it is likely that they will review the contents. Yet not all social media accounts are monitored closely and regularly and some accounts are mentioned by many for a wide variety of reasons. Responses are not guaranteed! Hashtags are useful for those who following a specific topic, while signifying the intended subject(s); at the same time, they are also effective tools to build a community, e.g. #ScholComm for scholarly communication researchers and practitioners.

Researchers and research institutions can engage and inform the public on social media platforms. Before launching a social media campaign, it is necessary to consider the ground rules: what kinds of content will be shared? How will the account be monitored? How to respond to negative and even malicious comments? Since social media posts are generally public, they can be responded to by individuals with a wide range of economic, political and religious interests and even trolls. Despite the potential setbacks, social media can serve as the bridge between researchers and practitioners, policymakers and the general public. A blog or a tweet can be very effective in bringing attention to research and scholarship that bring information and clarification on scientific and historical facts. As with any kinds of publications or communications, it is useful to consider who the intended audience are and also how social media posts can be interpreted or misunderstood.

Notwithstanding the benefits of social media, their use can create extra workload and stress for researchers. It is advisable for those who are new to a platform to observe and find their comfort zone, taking into account their professional identity, style of contributions and frequency of participation. If a researcher is uncomfortable participating in social media at a personal level, an alternative is to create a group or department account for sharing news and updates about publications, news and events, as well as public engagement activities.

Drawing boundaries: social media for academics

One of the most concerning issues for researchers participating in social media is the maintenance of professional identity. For those who have been on social media in a personal capacity, it is worth considering if a separate identity should be created: the existing social networks (following and followers) may not be interested in your research. Another consideration is whether it is fine for new connections to browse through your previous postings should they be curious enough. Would you be open to your employers, colleagues and students to know about your personal history? More importantly, a researcher should consider whether they plan to share their personal interests and opinions, or would they be only sharing and commenting in a professional capacity? Whatever a researcher presents themselves as on social media, it is important to bear in mind that the contents are publicly accessible, meaning that students, university management, journalists and many others can see and comment on your posts.

Managing a social media account can be time-consuming. It is a researcher's personal choice as to how much they devote to social media: while some are comfortable with the constant interactions and updates, others can find social media draining and distracting. At the bottom line, social media uses are beneficial as long as they empower researchers and enhance the visibility and impact of research. As in the everyday use of social media, some can become overly invested and there can also be problems of information overload. Mark Carrigan's *Social Media for Academics* (2020) provides a comprehensive overview for the best uses and practices.

Societal impact, social media and scholarly communication

Even though the planning of societal impact and the use of social media are not 'scholarly communication' in the strictest sense, they are now often embedded in the research planning process. Impact statements (or 'pathway to impact') in grant applications and the impact case studies method have called for more attention to the understanding and assessment of societal impact. Researchers are expected to articulate the potential societal impact of proposed projects and they are encouraged to showcase the benefits of research to society at large. Scholarly communication librarians and other research support roles can assist with the planning, monitoring and tracking of societal impact data, while they can also be involved in the development of research for policy.

Social media can be used for scholarly communication: journal clubs and live tweeting are good ways to network with researchers outside a researcher's own institution. They can also be used to promote publications and events. Social media platforms are vital for engaging a wider audience, for the postings can be shared and reposted by interested accounts from community organisations, journalists, to government agencies. Many research libraries are already supporting social media use by offering workshops about different platforms and digital identity.

8
Research Integrity

Introduction
Research integrity is concerned with the conduct and practices of researchers, involving issues pertaining to authorship, fabrication and falsification, paper mills and so on. The emergence of generative AI tools supported by machine learning, such as ChatGPT, has also raised questions about authenticity, copyright and the future of scholarly communication. Research integrity is of utmost importance, because research and researchers can only be trusted if research studies are conducted in good faith and if research articles are not used as a vehicle for peddling unsubstantiated facts and unjustified claims. The ethos of science, commonly known as 'Mertonian norms', proposed by the sociologist of science, Robert Merton (1973, originally published 1942), are as follows:

- Universalism: The acceptance or rejection of research findings is not dependent on personal or social attributes such as race, nationality, religion, class and personal qualities.
- Communism: The imperative for communication of findings is linked to the conception of science as part of the public domain, meaning that full and open communication shall form the basis of scholarly communication.
- Disinterestedness: The trust of scientific research is based on the disinterestedness of researchers rather than personal, commercial or political gains.
- Organised scepticism: Research data and scientific claims are open for scrutiny and subject to critique and revision.

The Mertonian norms speak to the basis on which the integrity and conduct of research should be upheld. On the one hand, research findings can be distorted if a research study is under commercial or political influence. On the other hand, it is problematic if the acceptance or rejection of a manuscript is affected by the personal or social attributes of an author, which can result in important research findings being neglected. Researchers are generally trusted to advance knowledge and conduct research for public good. In fact, research findings based on fabricated data or fraudulent practices can lead to dire consequences, especially when they are reported in the mass media. One infamous example is the false reporting of the MMR vaccine as a cause of autism. Although the research article was eventually retracted, the reporting has been part of the anti-vaccination discourse. Worse, the reports of misconduct can lead to distrust in researchers and research institutions.

In recent years, there have been increased reports of fraudulent research and retraction. Some argue that misconduct and manipulation in research are largely due to the intense pressure of research assessment, pointing to the overemphasis on the number of publications and citations in applications for academic positions, tenure and promotion and research grants (Biagioli and Lippman, 2020). In some countries, publications are required for a doctorate degree, whilst others reward publications with monetary rewards. As a result, most research integrity issues are related to the inflation of the number of publications and citations. The importance of research integrity in scholarly communication and knowledge production cannot be neglected. This chapter provides an overview of topics including authorship, attribution of credits, fabrication and falsification, alongside with descriptions of retraction, paper mills and generative AI, followed by a discussion of the responsibility of researchers, librarians and universities in upholding research integrity.

A note on research ethics

Research ethics is about the protection of research subjects, human and animals, in the process of research. It is particularly important for vulnerable subjects, for example children and elderly and marginalised groups. Research ethics guidelines are to ensure that no unnecessary harm is done to the research subjects, physical or psychological, and that informed consent will be acquired and compensation made when necessary. While research ethics is an important topic, it is distinguished from research integrity, which is concerned with the conduct of researchers and the writing and publication of research.

Authorship

Who is an author? A simple answer is that the person who writes a manuscript. Authorship is usually not a complicated matter in the humanities and social sciences because most works are composed by sole authors, or are co-written by two or three authors. For co-authored works, most would assume that the lead author is the main author or contributor unless otherwise stated. Authorship in the STEM (science, technology, engineering and mathematics) disciplines can be more complicated, for two main reasons: first, authors are alphabetically ordered in some disciplines, meaning that it is impossible to distinguish the lead author; secondly, the number of authors tends to be higher and hyperauthorship has become a norm in the so-called 'big team' science (Nogrady, 2023). Notwithstanding the varied norms and practices, research integrity issues arise when a name is listed as an author although the individual did not contribute to a research study or the writing of a manuscript. Ghost authorship and gift authorship are the two most discussed in the context of research integrity.

Ghost authorship
Ghost authorship means that a manuscript is written by 'ghost authors', meaning that the actual writers are not listed as authors and the listed authors did not actually write the article. Reports of ghost authorship have been mostly in clinical practice, where clinicians are required to publish for career advancement but do not have sufficient time to write up their research. In these cases, ghost writers are paid to write the research articles.

Reports of ghost authorship also include cases where early-career researchers (ECRs), including PhD students, draft manuscripts for senior researchers but their contributions are not acknowledged in the published article. In other words, they are not listed as an author and they also cannot claim credits or recognition for their work. Other instances can include articles produced by paper mills, which will be discussed later in the chapter.

Ghost authorship means that the listed authors do not write the article. In some disciplines, it is considered a questionable practice, given that the listed authors did conduct the research and reviewed and revised a manuscript before submission. In cases where ECRs are not attributed authorship, reported cases can be considered as misconduct and a violation of authorship policy. However, these cases are not usually disclosed, because ECRs are wary of repercussions that can affect their career progression, especially when many are on precarious contracts. Both forms of ghost authorship are not easy to detect, yet implementation of authorship policy can offer clear guidelines for both senior and early-career researchers.

Gift authorship
Gift authorship means that authors are credited as authors even though they are not involved in a research study or the writing of a manuscript. Gift authors can be listed for various reasons: one is to increase the visibility of an

article due to the gift authors' repute, with the goal of increasing the number of readers and, potentially, citations of an article. Gift authorship is also often attributed to senior researchers and principal investigators of a research project, although they are not directly involved in a specific study or the writing of a manuscript. This practice can be due to the power dynamics in a research group, whilst it can also involve the key reason for gift authorship: to increase visibility and readership of an article.

The inclusion of gift authors is usually considered a form of gaming. It is difficult to discern if a suspected gift author has contributed to a manuscript, or whether it would be considered malpractice if they did review and comment on a manuscript. There are also questions as to who should take the blame and who should be more liable: those who invite gift authors or those who accept the authorship without contributions. As in the case of ghost authorship, raising awareness and the implementation of authorship policy are helpful in shaping a better research culture.

Plagiarism and self-plagiarism

The Oxford English Dictionary definition of plagiarism is 'the practice of taking someone else's work or ideas and passing them off as one's own'. Essentially, an individual plagiarises another author's work when they use a sentence, a paragraph or a concept without attributing to the original work. There are also cases where an entire article or book is plagiarised. Compared to ghost authorship or gift authorship, plagiarism is treated as a serious misconduct in scholarly publications. Plagiarism is also easier to identify and track by tools on submission platforms; they can also be spotted by researchers and readers who can present clear evidence.

It is obvious that stealing others' work cannot be tolerated, even if not punished. There are, however, occasions when editors will take into account cultural and epistemic traditions. For example, some researchers from non-Western countries are educated to recite established scholars' work as a way of expressing respect. In these cases, an editor can request proper quotations and citations before the accusation of plagiarism. There are also different considerations for translated works. Translations are not plagiarised works because the author(s) of the original work are attributed as the author(s), alongside with the name(s) of the translator(s). Problems arise, however, when an individual uses translated contents and passes them as their own. Although it is not the typical 'copy and paste', using translated contents without attributing to the original works is considered plagiarism. However, these cases are often difficult to detect.

Then what is self-plagiarism? It seems quite odd to say that an author steals their own work and passes it off as their own! Why can't an author reuse their own materials? In the context of scholarly communication, the considerations of self-plagiarism are not about the attribution of the original work, but the claiming of credits for a piece of writing, because the number of publications is often used as a proxy for research performance. It is not acceptable to list multiple publications which are essentially the same piece of work as a false impression of of productivity. From the perspective of publishers, the reuses of texts are problematic, as that can affect readership and marketability of their publications. However, it is possible to reuse materials when agreed by an editor or a publisher. The extent to which a text, a paragraph, or a few sentences can be reused can be negotiated with the editor-in-chief of a journal or the managing editor of a publisher. When submitting a manuscript, an author can indicate the reuse of the materials in the covering letter, noting the reasons and the original source. The editor can then decide whether it is appropriate, or they can advise rewriting. It is increasingly common for conference organisers to negotiate the publication of conference papers in a special issue of a journal, given the submissions are substantially expanded versions of the papers. At times book publishers are also willing to publish a collection of essays or articles previously published. In these cases, the authors certainly would not be accused of self-plagiarism, as it is the publisher's decision that there are added values to republish the materials.

Attribution of credits
Authorship can be discussed from many perspectives, taking into consideration disciplinary differences and epistemic norms. In the context of research integrity, it is primarily about the claiming of credits. Ghost authorship, gift authorship and plagiarism are all about claiming undeserved credits. It is generally understood that these practices are a consequence of the chase after research metrics, that is, the number of publications and citations. The fine line between acceptable and questionable practices can be difficult to draw in some instances. In response to these challenges, CRediT: Contributor Roles Taxonomy (NISO, n.d.) has been developed and it has been implemented in some journals. The 14 contributor roles are:

1 Conceptualisation: Ideas; formulation or evolution of overarching research goals and aims
2 Data curation: Management of activities to annotate (produce metadata), scrub data and maintain research data (including software code, where it is necessary for interpreting the data itself) for initial use and later reuse
3 Formal analysis: Application of statistical, mathematical, computational or other formal techniques to analyse or synthesise study data

4 Funding acquisition: Acquisition of the financial support for the project leading to this publication
5 Investigation: Conducting a research and investigation process, specifically performing the experiments, or data/evidence collection
6 Methodology: Development or design of methodology; creation of models
7 Project administration: Management and co-ordination responsibility for the research activity planning and execution
8 Resources: Provision of study materials, reagents, materials, patients, laboratory samples, animals, instrumentation, computing resources, or other analysis tools
9 Software: Programming, software development; designing computer programs; implementation of the computer code and supporting algorithms; testing of existing code components
10 Supervision: Oversight and leadership responsibility for the research activity planning and execution, including mentorship external to the core team
11 Validation: Verification, whether as a part of the activity or separate, of the overall replication/reproducibility of results/experiments and other research outputs
12 Visualisation: Preparation, creation and/or presentation of the published work, specifically visualisation/data presentation
13 Writing – original draft: Preparation, creation and/or presentation of the published work, specifically writing the initial draft (including substantive translation)
14 Writing – review and editing: Preparation, creation and/or presentation of the published work by those from the original research group, specifically critical review, commentary or revision – including pre- or post-publication stages.

The taxonomy is useful for identifying the contribution of individuals and their roles in a research project. To a certain extent, it can also resolve issues related to ghost and gift authorship. At the same time, CRediT is a way of ascribing liability to responsible persons. For example, an author who writes a literature review is not necessarily accountable for data collection and analysis. Some journals now require the declaration of authorship, while many authors also voluntarily include statements of responsibility in their manuscripts.

Paper mills

Paper mills are commercial entities that generate manuscripts and sell authorship. They submit manuscripts to journals like any other authors and once a manuscript has been accepted for publication, the authorship is put up for sale on their website. The prices of authorship are determined by two factors: the impact factor (or similar) of the journal and the position of the author. Paper mills are not usually readily findable by using search engines, though they are active in some social networks. Some paper mills even place targeted advertisements on social media platforms.

Retraction Watch (https://retractionwatch.com), a blog report on retractions of scientific papers and related topics, revealed the working of a paper mill, International Publisher LLC, where Clarivate's Web of Science found 344 articles available for sale (Perron, Hiltz-Perron and Victor, 2019). The diverse set of strategies International Publisher LLC used to promote fraudulent publications included ghost-writing services, fake peer reviews and peer-review rings. Further, they found that paper mill articles were often associated with special issues.

Articles produced by paper mills pose significant threats to knowledge production and scholarly communication. Many of these articles are accepted based on fake peer reviews, meaning that the articles are reviewed by 'recommended reviewers' who can be the 'authors' themselves with a different e-mail address or someone with a conflict of interest. There are also 'peer-review rings', that is, peer reviewers who accept each other's manuscripts. As a result, the accepted articles do not necessarily meet the quality standards and, in some cases, there can be serious mistakes. Yet, paper mill articles are not always detectable once they are published, despite some high-profile cases that result in retraction and delisting of journals.

The Committee on Publication Ethics (COPE) has published a report (COPE and STM, 2022) that details the working mechanisms of paper mills and provides recommendations that are useful for detecting paper mill submissions. One important sign of paper mill articles is the changes in authorship after an article has been accepted, indicating an article could have been 'on sale'. The report also suggests that the lack of institutional affiliation and institutional e-mail address can be indicative, although it should be taken into account that independent researchers are not affiliated with an institution and that some institutions do not have institutional e-mail addresses.

Reproducibility

Reproducibility is a principle that underpins the scientific method: researchers should be able to reproduce consistent results using the same data, experiments or codes in an original study. In other words, the results and conclusions of a study can be verified and validated through direct replication and reanalysis. In the National Academies of Sciences, Engineering and Medicine Consensus Study Report (2019), *reproducibility* is defined as 'computational replicability', meaning that consistent results can be obtained by using the same data, computational steps, methods, code and conditions of analysis. A related concept is *replicability*, which involves obtaining consistent results across studies that address the same research questions with their own set of data. We focus on reproducibility in the discussion of research integrity.

The emphasis on reproducibility is a significant step that can tackle problems related to fraudulent research and paper mills. If the results of a research study are not reproducible, how can we trust the results and the conclusions? True, there can be honest mistakes discovered after an article has been published. These mistakes can occur in the process of data collection, computational steps, methods or code. When research findings are not reproducible, it is important to find out what went wrong. It is not a matter of research integrity so long as the researchers are open and transparent about their data and methods. However, it is a research integrity issue in cases where data were fabricated and/or the findings were falsified. Fabrication means that the data, images or results are 'made up', whereas falsification involves the manipulation of research materials, data or processes to achieve the desired results. Fabricated data and images are not always detectable during the editorial or peer-review processes; as a result, unverifiable results can be published and retained on the scholarly record.

The online journal club PubPeer (https://pubpeer.com) provides a platform for the discussion of suspected cases of fabricated data and images. Some journals also recruit image checkers to flag possible fraud. However, these mechanisms are insufficient to confront research integrity issues, due to the vast number of submissions, including those produced by paper mills. This is one major reason behind the call for open data and open code, since reproducibility is the key to countering fabrication and falsification in research. The National Academies of Sciences, Engineering and Medicine (2019) recommends that researchers should include clear, specific and complete information about any computational methods and data products that support their published results, as well as a description of how the reported result was reached. In addition to best practices of open research, it is necessary to undertake the replication and fact-checking process for verifying results. The goal of reproducible research demands changes in research culture: one that encourages and motivates the publication of replication studies, statistically non-significant results and negative results. It is also necessary to invest in the development of open-source tools and open infrastructure for sustainable and collaborative research. Researchers must be recognised and rewarded for their work in replication studies.

Retraction

Retraction means that an article is withdrawn after it has been published. The decision to retract is made by the editorial board and can be initiated by the author(s) or editor(s). If only a portion of an article is retracted, an article is labelled as a corrected article or a new version, depending on the functionalities of the publication platform. Retraction can be seen as a self-correcting mechanism in research: when errors and mistakes are found, the research findings cannot be used as the basis on which future research studies can be designed and they should no longer be on the scholarly record.

Retraction is not synonymous with fraud or failure. It is not uncommon that errors and mistakes are spotted after an article has been published. Honest mistakes should be corrected or retracted. However, it can be a difficult decision when the number of publications can make or break a researcher's career, even though burying the mistakes is counterproductive to scientific research. A cultural shift is needed to encourage and destigmatise honest mistakes. In 2020, for example, the Nobel Laureate Frances Arnold retracted a paper published in *Science* because the results were not reproducible and the authors found data missing from a lab notebook (BBC, 2020). Retracting the article was the right thing to do. This example speaks to the importance of reproducibility, the necessity to support replication and reanalysis and the need to normalise retraction.

Nevertheless, retractions also occur because of research misconduct, including the fabrication and falsification of data, falsification of results and plagiarism. These problems are usually reported by researchers, as well as sleuths who devote their work to detecting and spotting fraudulent research (Shen, 2020). For instance, two articles were retracted from the most prominent journals *The Lancet* and *The New England Journal of Medicine* due to questionable data sources during the Covid-19 pandemic (Piller and Servick, 2020). The retraction was a collective effort by researchers who read and scrutinised the articles post-publication. The PubPeer platform has been noted as a safe space for raising alarms and discussing potential frauds.

Other reasons that can lead to retraction are related to authorship and paper mills, including forged authorship, fake peer reviews and failure to disclose competing or conflict of interests. Recent cases show the extent to which paper mill articles have become a major cause of retraction. For example, the Institute of Physics (IOP) retracted nearly 1,000 articles in 2022 that are likely paper mill papers, citing the following indicators of manipulation (Oransky, 2022a, 2022b):

- Nearly all papers in both volumes contain more than one unrelated reference to the conference organiser's work and others at the organiser's institutions (many of whom are authors in the proceedings).
- Authors report having work accepted immediately and receiving no peer review reports.
- High level of similarity between manuscripts.
- Some papers have significant overlap with other papers published around the same time, by different authors.
- Some papers contain tortured phrases, masking high levels of plagiarism.
- Similarities in the content and format of peer review reports.

Retraction is an important mechanism for correcting the scholarly record. Retraction can occur because of honest mistakes and it is not always an indicator of misconduct and manipulation. Unfortunately, the term has become associated with fraudulent research, due to the research misconduct and the proliferation of paper mills.

Generative AI: chatbots and more

The arrival of ChatGPT in late 2022 has sparked many discussions about research integrity in the context of scholarly communication. The tool enables researchers to create texts by keyword prompts and links to relevant literature. Unlike plagiarised contents, ChatGPT can generate different texts, especially when prompted by specific questions. It is generally agreed that it will be very difficult or simply a waste of effort to detect the use of generative AI such as ChatGPT, especially when more powerful large language models (LLMs) are expected to be used in the near future. The question is: is it ethical or acceptable to use such tools for generating scholarly publications? If so, can ChatGPT be listed as an author?

Some researchers are supportive of these tools because they can improve the quality of writing, especially for those who are not the best writers and those who are non-native English speakers. The issues concerning authorship are controversial, however. Similar to the discussions about self-driving cars and similar technologies, there lies the question of responsibility and accountability: generative AI cannot be held responsible for the contents it generates. The publisher Springer Nature has already forbidden ChatGPT to be listed as an author (Nature Editorial, 2023).

Editorial and peer-review tools assisted by artificial intelligence have also sparked discussions about the future of scholarly publishing recently. For example, should they be used for screening a text and determining whether it fits the scope and objectives of a journal by detecting key words and references? Should they be used to select peer reviewers automatically?

Although these tools can facilitate the process by significantly reducing the effort of editors and peer reviewers, there are worries that they will reproduce biases. It is because these tools have been developed using existing corpuses, that is, the vast body of literature predominantly produced in Western countries and presumably the majority by white males. The development of generative AI and its appropriate and inappropriate uses will be an important topic in scholarly communication as the capabilities, functionalities and implications of these tools unfold.

Research integrity and scholarly communication

Research integrity underlies the trustworthiness of research and scholarship: fabricated or falsified results can become misleading evidence for future studies, while reports of researchers' misconduct can lead to distrust of researchers and research institutions. Fraudulent research can become a source of disinformation that can influence public opinion and political decisions and some can lead to dire consequences. Ultimately, there is no place for bad information and false claims. It is understandable that research does not always go as expected (which is the very reason for research!) and there can be honest mistakes. Retraction is a good mechanism for notifying the research community about errors and corrections. Those who are honest should be applauded and supported. In this sense, retraction should not be stigmatised. Unfortunately, most retractions occur because of significant misconduct, but fixing the problems related to research integrity is not only about the individuals, but also systemic changes in research assessment and relevant policies.

The many issues discussed in this chapter concern the conduct of researchers – claiming authorship without contributing to a manuscript or a research study, buying authorship from paper mills, making up data and results, or stealing images from previous studies and passing them on as their own. There is no question that researchers are responsible when it comes to research integrity. In fact, paper mills cannot survive if they have no customers. Yet it is important to understand the reasons behind research misconduct and manipulation and many have pointed to the overemphasis on research metrics, including the number of publications and citations (Chapter 6). Publication in a high-impact journal as a requirement for graduation can lead to the use of paper mills by early-career researchers. The so-called 'publish or perish' culture is unconducive to research integrity and even a perverse incentive, especially where researchers may be rewarded by cash bonuses.

The Committee on Publication Ethics was founded in 1997 and has since provided best practice and guidance for publishers and other actors in the scholarly communication landscape. Publishers as gatekeepers of scholarly information play an important role in tackling research integrity issues such as forged authorship, fake peer review and paper mills. Some may argue that when publishers are doing their work properly, paper mill articles should not have gone through the editorial and peer-review process and fraudulent research should have been spotted. However, not every editor or reviewer has been advised about the widespread research integrity issues related to fabrication, falsification and paper mills. The picture becomes more complicated when some gold open access journals are predatory, in the sense that they are profit-maximising with little or no concern for quality or integrity because they do not depend on readership or subscription as an income source. To tackle issues from plagiarism to paper mills, a concerted effort by all actors in the scholarly communication landscape is required. Guidelines and best practices, systemic changes in research assessments and the move to open research are all contributing factors in maintaining research integrity in research.

9

Critical Issues and the Future of Scholarly Communication

Introduction

Scholarly communication is a fast-moving area. It is partly because digital publishing has now become predominant: when scholarly information is no longer confined within the bricks and mortar of academic libraries, new publishers emerge and challenge the status quo of academic publishing and scholarly communication. Open access advocates negotiate the ways by which commercial and public interests can be balanced, involving the development of scholar-led diamond open access journals, for-profit and non-profit gold open access journals and hybrid journals with gold open access options. Digital publishing also enables alternative ways of communicating research not confined to traditional academic publications, evident by the increased number of preprints, blogs, podcasts, videocasts and social media posts. The emergence of new publishers and non-traditional publication channels means that changes in research assessment criteria are necessary to determine what can be counted as research outputs and how they will be recognised and rewarded, not to mention the tension between best practices of open research and the expectations of publishing in established 'high-impact' journals. There are also concerns about copyright and licensing options that can result in changes in the intellectual property policy of universities and research institutions. Together, digital publishing enables faster dissemination of and open access to scholarly information. However, it has also initiated reconsideration and reconfiguration of many assumptions and questions in the scholarly communication landscape, concomitant with socio-technological and political changes involving the wide use of social media and the necessity of societal impact. The different configurations have implications for the academic publishing market, research dissemination and of course, the work of research support in scholarly communication.

The role of scholarly communication in research support is exhilarating and challenging. It is a position where a librarian is not only supporting researchers in the many aspects of scholarly communication from consultation services on publishing to the use of social media, but can also involve advocacy work in open access, research assessment and copyright reform. Some also develop and establish library publishing and similar initiatives. The work of scholarly communication librarians is primarily to support researchers to select the best venues for research dissemination for enhancing research and societal impacts, while it is also important to note that the choices made as to where to publish actively shape the academic publishing market and the scholarly communication landscape. In this chapter, we discuss some of the critical issues concerning academic publishing and knowledge production, followed by some thoughts about the future of scholarly communication.

Oligopolistic publishers

The majority of academic publications are products of commercial publishers, five of which have been nicknamed the 'Big Deals' due to their dominant market share. The 2019 Big Deals Survey Report (Morais, Stoy and Borrell-Damián, 2019) shows that the publishers Elsevier, Springer Nature, Wiley, Taylor & Francis and American Chemistry Society (ACS) published over 50% of the total number of publications, costing more than 75% of the total spent by subscription-fee-paying research institutions and libraries on academic journals in Europe, with a median price per article range from 1,344 to 2,658 (Table 9.1). It has also been reported that the subscription fees of their publications have increased at rates higher than inflation, with the expectation that there will be continuous growth in the number of journals in the future (Bhosale, 2022).

Table 9.1 *Price per article median value* (Source: Morais, Stoy and Borrell-Damián, 2019)

Publisher	Median	Average
Elsevier	€2,642	€3,476
Springer Nature	€1,344	€1,689
Wiley	€2,658	€2,577
Taylor & Francis	€1,509	€1,509
ACS	€2,570	€3,067

Furthermore, of particular interest are the extra revenue streams introduced via the gold open access option in hybrid journals. Notably, the biggest publishers are charging higher APCs compared to smaller publishers (Table 9.2 opposite). In other words, academic publishing is a big business for a small number of publishers, to the extent that they are considered an oligopoly. The dominance of these publishers is reinforced by the fact that their publications tend to be indexed on major databases, while new

Table 9.2 *Average price per article (APC) of OA journals by publisher size* (Source: https://waltcrawford.name/goa6.pdf CC BY)

Publisher	Journals	Articles	% No-fee	$/article
Largest: 600+	299	405,094	8%	$2,070
Large: 150-599	989	212,389	22%	$1,328
Medium: 60-149	2,980	204,847	55%	$537
Small: 20-59	7,962	210,220	75%	$204
Smallest: 0-19	2,968	28,706	82%	$125

publications are excluded due to the lack of a track record. The more submissions they receive, the better they can maintain the status quo.

There are two key issues: one is that the oligopolistic publishers can form a cartel, meaning that they can set subscription fees and article-processing charges much higher than a natural market price. This can substantially put pressure on library budgets because when a higher percentage of the budget is going to the Big Deals publishers, limited funds are left to support smaller ones, cementing the power of the oligopoly in the academic publishing market. The dominance of a few publishers is particularly problematic in light of the reported profit margin of RELX, the parent company of Elsevier, at 31.3% for 2018, a rate higher than that of major internet companies such as Apple and Google. Secondly and relatedly, reduced library budgets can lead to discontinued subscriptions to smaller publishers. Without subscriptions, it will become not viable for many small publishers to operate, despite their values, mission and quality. The closure of small publishers entails the consolidation of power of the big publishers and their expanding influences on knowledge production.

The recent reports about the Big Deals (Morais, Stoy and Borrell-Damián, 2019; Stoy, Morais and Borrell-Damián, 2019) and reports of price per article and their revenues (Crawford, 2021) have raised concerns about the future of scholarly publishing, including the financial burden placed upon library budgets by oligopolistic publishers. Some have called for diverting library budgets to support open research infrastructure (Lewis, 2017; Lewis et al., 2018), while others have developed or are developing library publishing programmes.

Platformisation: datafication and commodification

Scholarly communication has become a primarily online activity: most researchers conduct their searches and read articles online, they organise their bibliography using a reference manager, they upload articles and post comments to preprint servers. Meanwhile, a scholarly communication librarian may monitor and track the volume of publications and citations by collating indicators on various platforms; they can also produce benchmarking and other reports using a data analytic tool. Many of these products and tools used by researchers daily are owned by publishers or data analytic companies. Chen, Posada and Chan (2019) have shown the presence of Elsevier, for example, throughout the research, publishing and evaluation process. Their products include Mendeley, Plum X, Scopus, SciVal, SSRN and more.

The vertical integration means that some publishers are not only publishers; in fact, they offer products and services throughout the research lifecycle. This adds to the problems associated with the oligopolistic publishers: the situation in which knowledge production and scholarly communication are reliant, or over-reliant, on the commercial research infrastructure, particularly when these companies do not necessarily have the best interests of researchers or knowledge production as their highest priority, for the very reason that their business model is to maximise profits (Ma, 2023a). More worrying, however, is that some of these products are 'spying' on researchers, that is to say, they are tracking and recording activities when researchers conduct searches, viewing and highlighting an article and their interactions when using their tools and products (Wood, 2015; DFG, 2021). Similar to the data collection on many social media platforms, these data are collected and can be repackaged for sale.

On the one hand, these products infringe personal privacy and there seem to be no regulations that can restrict the data collection. Researchers sign the terms and conditions without reading them – for they usually do not have alternative options when accessing scholarly publications. From the perspective of a library, however, these spying activities violate the core values of information privacy (Ma, 2023b). Even though the library does not collect, store or process these data, it is necessary to protect the privacy of library users by examining and negotiating terms and conditions when subscribing to products and platforms.

On the other hand, these activities can lead to platformisation of scholarly information when data about research activities are being tracked and collected and then shared with or sold to third parties (Lamdan, 2023). Further, 'when platforms hold the dominating power in determining what kinds of information can be disseminated and rewarded and when informativeness is decoupled from the normative agreement or consensus co-constructed and co-determined in an open and public discourse' (Ma, 2023a, 280). The platformisation of scholarly information can lead to weakened negotiation powers of libraries to obtain, grant access to and preserve scholarly information.

Open research

Chapter 3 discusses the green, diamond and gold open access models from an author's perspective. For many authors, the open access model is secondary to the prestige or impact of a publisher or journal, due to the criteria of research assessment. Their key consideration is the dissemination of the publication and the number of citations it may attract. From a scholarly communication perspective, the choice of open access model offered by a publication can have a significant effect on the academic publishing market. For example, the more diamond open access journals are supported by high-quality submissions, the more likely it will become the dominant model of academic publishing. In other words, the choice of where to publish can actively shape the future of academic publishing. For one, supporting green and diamond open access publications can counter the over-reliance on the Big Deals publishers, while leaving room for smaller publishers to sustain and grow. It is also important to note that non-profit, scholar-led and library publishers are vital in the scholarly publishing ecosystem, because they tend to support emerging and marginalised voices. Indeed, the choice of open access option is one of the important decisions when it comes to the question: where to publish?

But open access is no longer limited to publications. The demand for reproducibility and replicability, combined with diverse research outputs, including datasets and codes, have called for open research (and sometimes referred to as 'open scholarship'), an umbrella term that encompasses open data, open source, open peer review, open methodology and open educational resources. Currently, there are different schools of thought when it comes to the openness of data, code, methodology and so on. They are influenced by disciplinary norms as well as issues pertaining to personal data protection and intellectual property. In many ways, open research is still in its infancy and there will be ongoing discussions and debates. As discussed in Chapter 5, for example, open peer review has various manifestations, each of which has its own pros and cons, as well as implications for researchers and publishers. Nevertheless, there is a general agreement that openness is beneficial for scholarly communication, knowledge production and public good. Specifically, openness is seen as an antidote to research integrity issues such as misconduct and manipulation discussed in Chapter 8.

Many funding agencies in Europe have adopted Plan S, meaning that the research outputs of funded projects must be made open-accessible with no embargo period. In the USA, the White House Office of Science and Technology Policy (OSTP) released a statement in 2022 that a policy will be in place to ensure research findings to be made available to the public with no delay or barriers (White House, 2022). The independent report commissioned by the European Commission (Johnson and European

Commission, 2022) shows the significance of a non-profit publishing service, Open Research Europe (ORE). Meanwhile, there are ongoing projects including DARIAH (Digital Research Infrastructure for the Arts and Humanities), OPERAS (Open Scholarly Communication in the European Research Area for Social Sciences and Humanities) and DIAMAS (Developing Institutional Open Access Publishing Models to Advance Scholarly Communication). Advocacy organisations such as SPARC and Confederation of Open Access Repositories have been providing guidance and drafting reports on the development of open-research infrastructure.

Research assessment reform

It has become clear that, however, open research will not be possible without research assessment reform. It is because current research assessment primarily, if not only, recognises positive results published in traditional, high-impact journals. The pressure to publish original research findings is a barrier for making their data and codes available for others to replicate and to reuse in future studies. Unless 'research outputs' such as data and codes are properly recognised, researchers may find it risky that others can report findings and publish articles without acknowledging their work.

The significance of traditional, high-impact journals in research assessments also means that researchers, especially those in their early career or on precarious contracts, would be reluctant to support and publish in scholar-led or diamond open access journals. As noted, this will reinforce the market share of the big commercial publishers, while hampering the development of open-research infrastructure. Further, it is also reasonable to argue that some research integrity issues can be addressed by research assessment reform. When researchers are not under immense pressure to publish, it is less likely that they will fabricate data or falsify results or buy authorship from paper mills, for the very fact that all these activities and manipulation are for increasing the number of publications. Ceasing the chase after research metrics is also important for countering data cartels (Lamdan, 2023) and the platformisation of scholarly information (Ma, 2023a, 2023b).

Most recently, the drafting of the Agreement on Reforming Research Assessment was initiated in January 2022, involving 350 organisations from over 40 countries. The Coalition for Advancing Research Assessment (CoARA) has over 500 signatories at the time of writing. The signatories include research institutions, funding agencies, scholarly associations, learned societies and national and regional authorities and agencies. CoARA is seen as a significant development, due to the fact that research assessment is at the crux of issues pertaining to open research (including open access) and research integrity.

For a scholarly communication librarian, keeping abreast of these developments is essential. Many who work in scholarly communication are advocates for research assessment reform. Their work involves promoting and implementing principles of DORA or the Leiden Manifesto and drafting institutional statements of responsible research metrics. They can also offer workshops and educational resources to share the knowledge about the proper uses and limitations of research metrics. Yet, while it is important to advocate for positive changes in the scholarly communication landscape, a pragmatic approach is appropriate and acceptable, particularly when assisting early-career researchers in forming their research dissemination strategy.

Bibliodiversity, multilingualism and sustainability

The concept of bibliodiversity, introduced in Chapter 3, is used to signify the importance of cultural and linguistic diversity of scholarly information, especially from a global perspective. Currently, the majority of scholarly publications are published by authors affiliated with institutions in Europe and North America. A study of publication trends by (World Bank) income level in the DOAJ shows that authors in low-income countries accounted for just over 1% of articles published in DOAJ journals in 2020 (Druelinger and Ma, in press). Many have commented that the gold open access model, or the introduction of APCs, will exacerbate the imbalance between high-, middle- and low-income countries (Nabyonga Orem et al., 2020; Berger, 2021).

What is the crux of the issue with regard to bibliodiversity? Firstly, some argue that bibliodiversity is challenged by the limited coverage and linguistic diversity of WoS and Scopus: while they are trusted as the gatekeepers of scholarly information, there are doubts about the selection criteria of non-Western and non-English-language publications. In other words, most publications indexed on the two major commercial databases are in English and non-English-language journals and books constitute a very small percentage. The limited coverage in turn 'delegitimises' journals published in other regions, languages and epistemic cultures because their selection criteria are regarded as the gold standard internationally.

Secondly, researchers based in countries outside Europe and North America are incentivised to publish in WoS- and Scopus-indexed publications. A journal does not have a JIF if it is not indexed on WoS. Likewise, citations from journals not indexed on Scopus will not count towards any metrics provided on the platforms. While they attempt to publish in English-language 'international' journals, they forgo 'local' publications in their own languages. This can lead to a diminishing number of journals in these regions, while research topics become tailored to international audiences rather than local interests.

And thirdly, the potential biases in peer review against authors who are affiliated with non-Western institutions mean that their manuscripts are less likely to be published in 'international' journals, not to mention that topics of interest in the African continent or Southeast Asian countries may seem irrelevant. It has been noted that some journals are considered 'predatory' for reasons unrelated to their quality, but because their concerns are seemingly irrelevant or unimportant from the predominantly Western perspectives upheld by these databases (Mills et al., 2021).

Together, these factors speak to the lack of bibliodiversity in the scholarly communication landscape, largely due to the overemphasis on research metrics provided by WoS and Scopus. The development of open-research infrastructures can counter some issues and promote bibliodiversity if the indexed journals are widely supported and 'counted' in research assessment. DOAJ and national indexes such as SciELO can be more prominent in representing research in all languages and of global and local interest. The Helsinki Initiative on Multilingualism in Scholarly Communication has three key recommendations (www.helsinki-initiative.org):

1 Support dissemination of research results for the full benefit of the society.
2 Protect national infrastructures for publishing locally relevant research.
3 Promote language diversity in research assessment, evaluation and funding systems.

To promote bibliodiversity and multilingualism, it is necessary to recognise publications not indexed on WoS and Scopus in research assessment so that researchers can be rewarded if they opt to publish in journals that are of national, regional and local relevance in their own language. This, in turn, can resolve some issues pertaining to research culture and research integrity due to the overemphasis and overuse of research metrics provided by the two major indexes.

Sustainable development goals (SDGs)

Bibliodiversity is important for global knowledge in enriching our understanding of nature, cultures and languages. Without initiatives to promote bibliodiversity, research around the world is not being shared and built upon and without purpose-built research infrastructures, valuable research findings are not preserved for discovery and access across space and time. Biases and exclusion in traditional 'international' journals become more pertinent when we consider sustainable development goals (SDGs), of which many challenges require research and understanding in different cultures and regions, because articles published in WoS- and Scopus-indexed journals can be irrelevant or inappropriate for resolving poverty and gender equality in non-Western countries, whereas research undertaken in non-Western countries may be rejected due to biases, conservatism or the lack of expertise in the peer-review process.

Here's an example that illustrates the problems of biases and exclusions. The Kenyan researcher Mary Abukutsa-Onyango is an expert in African indigenous crops. Her research had been rejected by prestigious international journals. She recalled, it was 'not because the research was not good, but because they regarded the crops I was writing about as weeds' (Badrudeen, 2022). When she went on to publish in an African journal, her research led to the development of nutrition schemes for schools in Kenya and the scheme was later adopted by East African governments. This example clearly illustrates that rejection by prestigious journals does not necessarily mean that the research is of insufficient quality or lower impact. Another astounding example is Katalina Karikó's work on mRNA, rejected by both *Nature* and *Science* and received little attention when it was finally published. Without extraordinary success in grant funding and publications, she was demoted by the University of Pennsylvania and eventually moved to industry. Dr Karikó's experience is likely not uncommon in today's hypercompetitive academic market, yet it is a clear indicator that very important research can sometimes be excluded or rejected.

Bibliodiversity and multilingualism can be sustained and thrive in an inclusive and diverse scholarly communication landscape. The predominance of a few commercial publishers, the overemphasis on research metrics and the gold open access model are barriers to the development of non-profit open-research infrastructure. Ultimately, bibliodiversity is vital for achieving SDGs and a better future. The work of scholarly communication librarians is not only research support in a narrow sense, but also involves education and advocacy, for the very reason that *where to publish* can shape the future of the scholarly communication landscape.

The future of scholarly communication

The key actors in the scholarly communication system – researchers and research communities, universities and research institutions, libraries, publishers, funders and policymakers – all play an important role in the development of infrastructures and policies that affect knowledge production and access to scholarly information. The Expert Group Report to the European Commission, *Future of Scholarly Publishing and Scholarly Communication* (European Commission, 2019), has identified important flaws in the scholarly publishing system and has recommended the following actions for practitioners and educators:

1 Organize and advocate free access to and right to reuse of publicly funded research results.
2 Reach out to funders, research institutions and policymakers in order to develop new communication channels, new forms of co-creation and co-planning of research and new forms of funding in response to needs, concerns and issues emanating from the population at large.
3 Look for opportunities to engage with research topics/results that are of interest to societal groups and their communities.
4 Bring forward research topics/questions that are mis- or under-represented (e.g. by contacting relevant researchers, attracting the attention of other actors in the science system or mobilising action in organised interest groups).

These recommendations provide guidance and support for scholarly communication libraries to address the issues and concerns related to open research, research assessment and bibliodiversity discussed.

In response to oligopolistic publishers and data tracking and surveillance, the article, 'The Platformisation of Scholarly Information and How to Fight It' (Ma, 2023b) proposes four actions to the research libraries community:

1 *Educate researchers about commercial publishers and APCs.* Researchers and university management are not usually informed about the business models of scholarly publishing and they have little, if any, knowledge about the budgetary issues faced by libraries. Most do not realise that the publishing in gold open access journals has implications for bibliodiversity and multilingualism. Educating researchers and university management about commercial publishing and APCs can stimulate conversations about the implications of different open access models and the necessity to support open research infrastructures.
2 *Allocate library budget to support scholar-led and library publishing and open infrastructure.* Research libraries with sufficient budgets can play a role in leveraging the powers of commercial publishers by allocating a small portion of budget to support open access programmes as suggested by the 2.5% commitment (Lewis 2017; Lewis et al., 2018). This can include library publishing, mission-driven new university presses and open textbook initiatives (Verbeke and Mesotten, 2022). Ensuring a budget for smaller publishers is also essential for maintaining a healthy scholarly publishing system.

3 *Engage in the development of public research infrastructures and copyright reform.* Public research infrastructures can ensure that the ownership of scholarly information remains in the hands of the public and that data privacy is respected in the context of scholarly communication. The development of public research infrastructures entails changes in copyright laws, including the first-sale doctrine and rights retention, affecting the provision of and access to information in research libraries.
4 *Advocate for research assessment reforms.* It is evident that research assessment has significant influences on research culture and research integrity. The chase after the number of publications and citations can be seen as a business strategy by commercial entities (Ma, 2023a), while obstructing the development of open research. The increasing instances of research misconduct and manipulation have been examined as a result of 'gaming the metrics' (Biagioli and Lippman, 2020). Research assessment reform is pressing for knowledge production and scholarly communication.

The future of scholarly communication is in flux. Each of the topics covered in this book addresses the basic knowledge required for understanding and navigating future changes. Guided by the question 'Where to publish?', the book invites the readers to examine and reflect on the pros and cons of publication types, open access and licensing options, appropriate and inappropriate uses of research metrics and the benefits and setbacks of peer review. All of these topics are 'moving parts' that can trigger changes in the future of scholarly communication. Put another way, it is pertinent that the decision as to where to publish is aligned with the values and norms of the research communities, libraries and other actors. These values and norms can evolve and are being negotiated over time. But if researchers and librarians are not knowledgeable or informed about the many little things involved in the publishing process and blindly follow the chase after metrics, then they may lose sight of the values and norms of research and can be rid of negotiating power in shaping the scholarly communication landscape. Changes in business models, library budgets, research assessment criteria, research policies, and funding mandates are imminent and ongoing. Yet, the biggest fundamental change is likely to be technological: there is no question that generative AI can transform how researchers conduct research, collect and analyse data and write manuscripts. It is premature to speculate the consequences and implications, but for sure it will be a steep learning curve in the near future.

Case studies

Much day-to-day work in research support is to develop educational materials and planning and delivering workshops. LibGuides provide the first contact point for researchers to find information about transformative agreements or copyright and intellectual property. Workshops (or a somewhat quaint term, 'bibliographic instruction') are organised to instruct in the use of platforms and tools and they also offer opportunities for interactions and questions which may lead to further consultation services. The complexities of scholarly publishing mean that answering questions about a topic (e.g. open access) usually involves advice on another (e.g. copyright and licensing). The following case studies are adapted from a 'Publishing and Dissemination Plan' assignment in a Scholarly Communication module. They are 'scenarios' where a researcher is seeking to develop a research dissemination plan and/or societal impact strategy, showcasing the interconnectedness of the topics covered in this book.

Case study 1 – Inter- or multi-disciplinary research

Sharon is a third-year doctoral student working at the intersection of Information Technology Law and Media Studies. Her thesis evaluates the fundamental rights and rule of law in relation to online disinformation regulation. She has been advised that she needs to publish at least two articles before graduation to be competitive on the job market. She has questions about publishing her work due to its inter- or multi-disciplinary nature. What would be the best ways to find scholarly publications that would be right for her career?

As inter- and multi-disciplinary research becomes common, Sharon's question is relevant to many. In her PhD studies, she reads and references works in the subject areas of information technology, communication and media and law. Where should Sharon aim to publish her work?

We can first use Scopus to find high-ranking journals in her research area. There are two relevant subject areas: 'Law' and 'Communication'. After browsing the two subjects, she decided that she will narrow her search to law journals on account of her use of a doctrinal legal research method.

The subject area 'Law' retrieves 1,013 results. The highest-ranked journal is *Government Information Quarterly*, which has a CiteScore of 14.5. Should Sharon aim to publish in this journal?

In Chapter 2, we discussed the scope and objectives of a journal and the importance of the intended audience. So, we'll advise Sharon to browse the journal website, including the 'About this journal' page. After a quick glimpse of the contents, it is apparent that Sharon's European focus is not represented in this journal. So she repeats these steps to select journals that are closest to her research topic and approach and finds 15 journals that publish articles which focus on European law and use a doctrinal legal research method (Table CS.1):

Table CS.1 *List of journals and their CiteScore and open access options*

Title	CiteScore	Percentile	Open Access
Computer Law and Security Review	6.2	97%	Gold (Hybrid)
International Journal of Law and Information Technology	4.2	94%	Gold (Hybrid)
Law, Innovation and Technology	3.5	92%	Gold (Hybrid)
Information and Communications Technology Law	3.4	91%	Gold (Hybrid)
International Review of Law, Computers and Technology	2.4	85%	Gold (Hybrid)
European Law Journal	2.0	80%	Gold (Hybrid)
International Journal of Human Rights	2.0	79%	Gold (Hybrid)
Modern Law Review	1.9	77%	No
Human Rights Review	1.7	74%	Gold (Hybrid)
Human Rights Law Review	1.6	73%	Gold (Hybrid)
Journal of Media Law	1.4	67%	Gold (Hybrid)
European Law Review	1.1	62%	No
Maastricht Journal of European and Comparative Law	1.1	62%	Gold (Hybrid)
Tilburg Law Review	0.7	45%	Diamond
European Public Law	0.8	50%	No

Sharon has heard about open access articles and is curious to learn more. When browsing the journals' websites, she noted that not every article was open access. As someone who is concerned about human rights, she believes that everyone should have equal rights to information access. She finds that the majority of journals offer open access options – one option is to pay an article-processing charge (APC), i.e. the gold option, and the other is self-archiving, i.e. the green option.

Which option should Sharon choose if she wants to make her publication open access? First, Sharon needs to find out if the APC is supported by a research grant or departmental funds, or if her library has signed a transformative agreement that covers the cost.

If there is no financial support or agreement in place, then she can consider the green open access option. In Chapter 3, we discussed that some publishers impose an embargo period before an author accepted manuscript (AAM) can be made publicly accessible. From Sharon's perspective, a shorter embargo period would be preferable.

Instead of the gold open access option in hybrid journals published by traditional commercial publishers, Sharon can consider *Tilburg Law Review*, which is a diamond open access journal that is free to read and free to publish. It is interesting to note that the three journals that do not offer an open access option are all society journals supported by subscription fees. They are fine options if Sharon's target audience is likely to be members of the professional society.

After browsing through these journals and noting their CiteScore and open access options, Sharon shared her findings with her supervisors and other PhD students. She was then advised that for legal academia, the prestige of a journal is also affected by its affiliation with well-known and highly ranked law schools; journals such as *Stanford Law Review*, *University of Pennsylvania Law Review*, *Yale Law Journal*. With this information in mind, Sharon again browses through the table of contents, open access policy and this time, she also looks into the author guidelines to get a better sense of the scope and types of publication.

Case study 2 – Preprints struggles

Lydia is a postdoctoral researcher in biomedical sciences. After receiving her PhD, she joined this research centre on a three-year individual fellowship. While she is formally mentored by a principal investigator, she is free to explore and investigate research topics of interest with the aim of landing a permanent position after the fellowship. To achieve her goal, she will need to have a solid track record of publications. She is an advocate of open research and it is commonplace to share preprints in her subject area. However, she has concerns about others scooping her research. She had a bad experience during her PhD studies when she was asked to be the ghost writer of several articles. What can Lydia do to protect her work – which can make or break her career – while also actively participating in the progress of open research?

It is very unfortunate that Lydia was treated as a ghost writer during her PhD study. Without clear guidelines and author policy, some researchers do not regard PhD students' work as substantial contributions to a research article. Some of these issues are discussed in Chapter 8. Scholarly communication librarians can play a role in promoting good research practices. It is essential to be fluent in the language of reproducibility and replication in the context of open research.

Let's think about Lydia's concerns about depositing her research outputs on preprint servers. It is very common for researchers in the field of biomedicine to share their research findings and even dataset and codes, on preprint servers. The reason is simple: the sooner they share their research outputs, the better for scientific progress. The Covid-19 health emergency has shown that making research openly accessible immediately is vital. But as an early-career researcher, Lydia is not very confident that her contributions will be acknowledged and worse, it can be 'scooped' by others without credits or attribution. She is also aware that the peer reviewers will know her identity when she submits the work to a journal.

In Chapter 5, we learnt that single-blind peer review is usual in STEM journals. Although the peer-review process can sometimes be biased, Lydia's concerns about the disclosure of identity cannot be avoided. In fact, depositing a preprint is more fruitful than harmful when it comes to potential biases because she is inviting feedback from the research community and not only the assigned peer reviewers. Alternatively, Lydia can also consider journals that facilitate open peer review – which can take the form of open identities, open reports and open interactions – which counter some of the problems with single-blind peer reviews while advocating open research practices. The interactions on these platforms can also build networks of potential collaborators.

Then how about Lydia's worries about scooping? Although scooping does happen, it should not preclude someone from depositing on peer review servers and other open research practices. Instead, Lydia can make use of scholarly social networks or blog posts to let others know about a preprint that is available. By doing so, she is taking responsibility for and promoting her work.

Case study 3 – Scholarly appeal and public audience

Cornelius is a historian who has written extensively about the conflicts and violence during the Great War. He has published five scholarly books and numerous articles and is an established scholar. Recently, he is contemplating writing a book for a general audience, while he is also hoping to enhance the public understanding of the relevance of historical research in policy making and politics. What does Cornelius need to consider when planning his publication and how can he enhance societal impact?

Cornelius is an experienced author. He is familiar with the process of writing a book proposal and pitching the unique contributions of his scholarly work. He also has contacts with prestigious university presses. Although they are not specialised in trade publications, some have imprints that are tailored for a general audience. Their publications – sometimes called 'crossover' – are available for purchase on most digital platforms and some book stores. Another option for Cornelius is to publish a trade book which can reach the general public through local and online bookstores. To publish a trade book, Cornelius may need to contact an agent as the first step.

The selection of a trade publisher is not dissimilar to scholarly publishing. Cornelius will find out if a publisher is supportive and helpful during the initial exchanges and book proposal process. He can also investigate the production, distribution and marketing by checking out publications by the same publisher, especially those that are in similar areas of study. Before signing a book contract, he will clarify the terms and conditions, including details about copyright, licence to publish and royalty payments. Alternatively, Cornelius can investigate if an open monograph is a viable option. He can consult the library if there is a library publishing programme and whether it publishes titles appropriate for a more general audience. If so, it can meet his ambition to share his work with anyone with internet access.

Whether he is publishing an open monograph, or a crossover or trade book with a small- or large-scale publisher, it is important that he retains the copyright and discerns the terms regarding the distribution and reuse of the contents, so that the materials can be used in any public engagement activities, promotion materials for podcasts and exhibitions and blogs and opinion pieces or columns in newspapers and magazines. As discussed in Chapter 4, authors sometimes can be negligent of the fact that they no longer own their publications and can infringe copyright law if they have signed away the copyright or granted an exclusive licence to publish.

Cornelius can then explore channels to engage with the public. As an established scholar, he can be invited to discuss timely topics on television, radio and podcasts. He can actively contact relevant media to discuss his new book by which he can demonstrate the significance of historical research in contemporary social and political contexts. He can also organise public talks, exhibitions, school visits and other outreach activities to invite public participation. Chapter 7 offers some prompts that are useful for planning activities for societal and policy impact. The first rule of thumb is to tailor the materials for the intended audience.

References

Adema, J. and Moore, S. A. (2021) Scaling Small; Or How to Envision New Relationalities for Knowledge Production, *Westminster Papers in Communication and Culture*, **16** (1), 27–45, https://doi.org/10.16997/wpcc.918.
ALLEA (2022) https://allea.org/allea-advocates-for-eu-wide-secondary-publication-rights-and-better-negotiation-of-future-big-deals.
Andrews, P. C. S. (2020) The Platformization of Open. In Eve, M. P. (ed.), *Reassembling Scholarly Communications*, 265–76, MIT Press, https://doi.org/10.7551/mitpress/11885.003.0027.
Badrudeen, A. (2022) How Africa is Overcoming 'Knowledge Colonialism', https://360info.org/how-africa-is-overcoming-knowledge-colonialism.
BBC (2020) Nobel Prize-Winning Scientist Frances Arnold Retracts Paper, www.bbc.com/news/world-us-canada-50989423.
Berger, M. (2021) Bibliodiversity at the Centre: Decolonizing Open Access, *Development and Change*, **52** (2), 383–404, https://doi.org/10.1111/dech.12634.
Bhosale, U. (2022) 2021 STM Report: Global Research Trends and Transformation in Open Access Publishing, www.enago.com/academy/2021-stm-report-global-research-trends.
Biagioli, M. and Lippman, A. (eds) (2020) *Gaming the Metrics: Misconduct and Manipulation in Academic Research*, MIT Press.
Blair, A. M. (2010) *Too Much to Know: Managing Scholarly Information Before the Modern Age*, Yale University Press.
BOAI (2002) Budapest Open Access Initiative, www.budapestopenaccessinitiative.org/read.
Buist-Zhuk, M. and Nieborg, M. (2022) A New University Press as a Space to Connect the Building Blocks of Open Science: A Look Through the Prism of an Open Textbook Publishing Pilot, Septentrio Conference Series, 1, https://septentrio.uit.no/index.php/SCS/article/view/6626.
Carrigan, M. (2020) *Social Media for Academics*, Sage.

Chan, L. (2019) Introduction. In Chan, L. and Mounier, P. (eds), *Connecting the Knowledge Commons: From Projects to Sustainable Architecture*, OpenEdition Press, https://books.openedition.org/oep/9050.

Chen, G., Posada, A. and Chan, L. (2019) Vertical Integration in Academic Publishing. In Chan, L. and Mounier, P. (eds), *Connecting the Knowledge Commons – From Projects to Sustainable Infrastructure*, OpenEdition Press, https://doi.org/10.4000/books.oep.9068.

Clarivate (n.d.-a) https://clarivate.com/webofsciencegroup/essays/impact-factor.

Clarivate (n.d.-b) Web of Science Journal Evaluation Process and Selection Criteria, https://clarivate.com/products/scientific-and-academic-research/research-discovery-and-workflow-solutions/web-of-science/core-collection/editorial-selection-process/editorial-selection-process.

Cleere, L. and Ma, L. (2018) A Local Adaptation in an Output-Based Research Support Scheme (OBRSS) at University College Dublin, *Journal of Data and Information Science*, **3** (4), 73–83, https://doi.org/10.2478/jdis-2018-0022.

CoARA (2022) *Agreement on Reforming Research Assessment*, https://coara.eu/app/uploads/2022/09/2022_07_19_rra_agreement_final.pdf.

COPE (2022) Avoiding Predatory Publishers, guest article, https://publicationethics.org/news/avoiding-predatory-publishers.

COPE, DOAJ ,OASPA and WAME (2022) Principles of Transparency and Best Practice in Scholarly Publishing (English), https://doi.org/10.24318/cope.2019.1.12.

COPE and STM (2022) Paper Mills: Research Report from COPE & STM (English), Committee on Publication Ethics. https://doi.org/10.24318/jtbG8IHL.

Cornish, G. P. (2019) *Copyright: Interpreting the Law for Libraries, Archives and Information Services*, Facet Publishing.

Cox, A. and Verbaan, E. (2018) *Exploring Research Data Management*, Facet Publishing.

Crawford, W. (2021) *Gold Open Access 2015–2020: Articles in Journals (GOA6)*, Cites and Insights Books.

Creative Commons (n.d.) https://creativecommons.org/choose.

Cronin, B. (2005) *The Hand of Science: Academic Writing and its Rewards*, Scarecrow Press.

Crossref (n.d.) www.crossref.org/services/cited-by.

Csiszar, A. (2018) *The Scientific Journal: Authorship and the Politics of Knowledge in the Nineteenth Century*, University of Chicago Press.

Daneshjou, R. and Adamson, A. S. (2020) Twitter Journal Clubs: Medical Education in the Era of social Media, *JAMA Dermatology*, **156** (7), 729–30, https://doi.org/10.1001/jamadermatol.2020.0315.

de Jong, S., Smit, J. and van Drooge, L. (2016) Scientists' Response to Societal Impact Policies: A Policy Paradox, *Science and Public Policy*, **43** (1), 102–14, https://doi.org/10.1093/scipol/scv023.

de Rijcke, S., Wouters, P. F., Rushforth, A. D., Franssen, T. P. and Hammarfelt, B. (2016) Evaluation Practices and Effects of Indicator Use: A Literature Review, *Research Evaluation*, **25** (2), 161–9, https://doi.org/10.1093/reseval/rvv038.

DFG (2021) Data Tracking in Research: Aggregation and Use or Sale of Usage Data by Academic Publishers. A briefing paper of the Committee on Scientific Library Services and Information Systems of the Deutsche Forschungsgemeinschaft (DFG, German Research Foundation), *Zenodo*, https://doi.org/10.5281/zenodo.5937995.

Druelinger, D. and Ma, L. (in press) Missing a Golden Opportunity? An Analysis of Publication Trends by Income Level in the Directory of Open Access Journals (DOAJ) 1987–2020, *Learned Publishing*.

Eglen, S. J. (2022) The Rights Retention Strategy (for Researchers), https://tiny.one/rrs-cam.

Elmore, S. A. and Weston, E. H. (2022) Predatory Journals: What They Are and How to Avoid Them, *Toxicologic Pathology*, **48** (4), 607–10, https://doi.org/10.1177/0192623320920209.

Elsevier (n.d.) www.elsevier.com/about/policies/copyright.

Emerald Group (2022) www.emeraldgrouppublishing.com/publish-with-us/author-policies/our-open-research-policies#green.

ESAC (n.d.) https://esac-initiative.org/about/transformative-agreements/agreement-registry.

European Commission (2019) *Future of Scholarly Publishing and Scholarly Communication: Report of the Expert Group to the European Commission*, Directorate-General for Research and Innovation, Publications Office of the European Union, https://data.europa.eu/doi/10.2777/836532.

European Commission (2023) Competence Framework 'Science for Policy' for Researchers. https://knowledge4policy.ec.europa.eu/visualisation/competence-framework-'science-policy'-researchers_en.

European Commission and Johnson, R. (2022) Operationalising Open Research Europe as a Collective Publishing Enterprise, Directorate-General for Research and Innovation, https://data.europa.eu/doi/10.2777/061886.

European Commission and Senftleben, M. R. F. (2022) Study on EU Copyright and Related Rights and Access to and Reuse of Data,

Directorate-General for Research and Innovation, Publications Office of the European Union, https://data.europa.eu/doi/10.2777/78973.

European Science Foundation (2012) The Challenges of Impact Assessment, http://archives.esf.org/coordinating-research/mo-fora/evaluation-of-publicly-funded-research.html.

Fair Open Access (n.d.) www.fairopenaccess.org/the-fair-open-access-principles.

Flaherty, C. (2022) The Peer-Review Crisis, www.insidehighered.com/news/2022/06/13/peer-review-crisis-creates-problems-journals-and-scholars.

Fyfe, A., Coate, K., Curry, S., Lawson, S., Moxham, N. and Røstvik, C. M. (2017) Untangling Academic Publishing: A History of the Relationship Between Commercial Interests, Academic Prestige and the Circulation of Research, *Zenodo*, http://doi.Org/10.5281/zenodo.546100.

Fyfe, A., Moxham, N., McDougall-Waters, J. and Røstvik, C. M. (2022) *A History of Scientific Journals: Publishing at the Royal Society, 1665–2015*, UCL Press.

Garcia, J. A., Rodriguez-Sánchez, R. and Fedez-Valdivia, J. (2020) Confirmation Bias in Peer Review, *Scientometrics*, **123**, 517–33, https://doi.org/10.1007/s11192-020-03357-0.

Garfield, E. (1955) Citation Indexes for Science, *Science*, **122**, 108–11.

Garfield, E. (1972) Citation Analysis as a Tool in Journal Evaluation, *Science*, **178**, 471–9.

Grudniewicz, A., Moher, D., Cobey, K. D., Bryson, G. L., Cukier, S., Allen, K., Ardern, C., Balcom, L., Barros, T., Berger, M., Buitrago Ciro, J., Cugusi, L., Donaldson, M. R., Egger, M., Graham, I. D., Hodgkinson, M., Khan, K. M., Mabizela, M., Manca, A., Milzon, K., Mouton, J., Muchenje, M., Olijhoek, T., Ommaya, A., Patwardhan, B., Poff, D., Proulx, L., Rodger, M., Severin, A., Strinzel, M., Sylos-Labini, M., Tamblyn, R., van Neikerk, M., Wicherts, J. M. and Lalu, M. M. (2019) Predatory Journals: No Definition, No Defence, *Nature*, **576**, 210–12, https://doi.org/10.1038/d41586-019-03759-y.

Hames, I. (2007) *Peer Review and Manuscript Management in Scientific Journals: Guidelines for Good Practice*, Blackwell Publishing.

Hicks, D. (2012) Performance-Based University Research Funding Systems, *Research Policy*, **41** (2), 251–61, https://doi.org/10.1016/j.respol.2011.09.007.

Hicks, D., Wouters, P., Woltman, L., de Rijcke, S. and Rafols, I. (2015) Bibliometrics: the Leiden Manifeto for Research Metrics, *Nature*, **520**, 429–31, https://doi.org/10.1038/520429a.

Hinchliffe, L. J. (2022) The State of the Version of Record, *Scholarly Kitchen*, https://scholarlykitchen.sspnet.org/2022/02/14/the-state-of-the-version-of-record.

Hirsch, J. E. (2005) An Index to Quantify an Individual's Scientific Research Output, *Proceedings of the National Academy of Sciences (PNAS)*, **102** (46), 16569–72, https://doi.org/10.1073/pnas.0507655102.

Horbach, S. P. and Halffman, W. (2020) Journal Peer Review and Editorial Evaluation: Cautious Innovator or Sleepy Giant?, *Minerva*, **58**, 139–61, https://doi.org/10.1007/s11024-019-09388-z.

Imaging Neuroscience (2023) https://imaging-neuroscience.org/Announcement.pdf.

Johnson, R. and European Commission, Directorate-General for Research and Innovation (2022) *Operationalising Open Research Europe as a Collective Publishing Enterprise*, Publications Office of the European Union, https://data.europa.eu/doi/10.2777/061886.

Johnson, R. T. and Dickersin, K. (2007) Publication Bias Against Negative Results from Clinical Trials: Three of the Seven Deadly Sins, *Nature Clinical Practice Neurology*, **3** (11), 590–1, https://doi.org/10.1038/ncpneuro0618.

Kellogg Foundation (2004) *Logic Model Development Guide: Using Logic Models to Bring Together Planning, Evaluation and Action*, www.aacu.org/sites/default/files/LogicModel.pdf.

Laakso, M., Matthias, L. and Jahn, N. (2021) Open is not Forever: A Study of Vanished Open Access Journals, *Journal of the Association for Information Science and Technology*, **72** (9), 1099–112, https://doi.org/10.1002/asi.24460.

Lamdan, S. (2023) *Data Cartels: The Companies That Control and Monopolize our Information*, Stanford University Press.

Lane, C. (2023) How to Use the QS World University Rankings by Subject, www.topuniversities.com/subject-rankings/methodology.

Lee, C. J., Sugimoto, C. R., Zhang, G. and Cronin, B. (2013) Bias in Peer Review, *Journal of the American Society for Information Science and Technology*, **64** (1), 2–17, https://doi.org/10.1002/asi.22784.

Lewis, D. W. (2017) The 2.5% Commitment, 2017, http://doi.org/10.7912/C2JD29.

Lewis, D. W., Goetsch, L., Graves, D. and Roy, M. (2018) Funding Community Controlled Open Infrastructure for Scholarly Communication: The 2.5% Commitment Initiative, *College & Research Libraries*, **79** (3), 133, https://doi.org/10.5860/crln.79.3.133.

Lippincott, S. K. (2016) The Library Publishing Coalition: Organizing Libraries to Enhance Scholarly Publishing, *Insights*, **29** (2), 186–91, http://doi.org/10.1629/uksg.296.

LSE Impact (n.d.) https://blogs.lse.ac.uk/impactofsocialsciences.

Ma, L. (2022) Metrics and Epistemic Injustice, *Journal of Documentation*, **78** (7), 392–404, https://doi.org/10.1108/JD-12-2021-0240.

Ma, L. (2023a) Information, Platformized, *Journal of Association for Information Science and Technology*, **74** (2), 273–82, https://doi.org/10.1002/asi.24713.

Ma, L. (2023b) The Platformisation of Scholarly Information and How to Fight It, *LIBER Quarterly*, **33** (1), https://doi.org/10.53377/lq.13561.

Ma, L. and Agnew, R. (2022) Deconstructing Impact: A Framework for Impact Evaluation in Grant Applications, *Science and Public Policy*, **49** (2), 289–301, https://doi.org/10.1093/scipol/scab080.

Ma, L., Buggle, J. and O'Neill, M. (2023) Open Access at a Crossroads: Library Publishing and Bibliodiversity, *UKSG Insights*, in press.

Ma, L., Luo, J., Feliciani, T. and Shankar, K. (2020) How to Evaluate *Ex Ante* Impact of Funding Proposals? An Analysis of Reviewers' Comments on Impact Statements, *Research Evaluation*, **29** (4), 431–40, https://doi.org/10.1093/reseval/rvaa022.

McGinnigle, E., Francis, R, Warriner, D. R. and McAloon, C. J. (2017) Journal Clubs in the Digital Age: Twitter for Continuing Professional Development, *Future Healthcare Journal*, **4** (3), 160–6, https://doi.org/10.7861/futurehosp.4-3-160.

McSherry, C. (2001) *Who Owns Academic Work: Battling for Control of Intellectual Property*, Harvard University Press.

Markie, M. L. (2015) Post Publication Peer Review, in All Its Guises, is Here to Stay, *Insights*, **28** (2), 107–10, http://doi.org/10.1629/uksg.245.

Martin, B. R. (2011) The Research Excellence Framework and the 'Impact Agenda': Are We Creating a Frankenstein Monster?, *Research Evaluation*, **20** (3), 247–54.

Merton, R. K. (1973) *The Sociology of Science: Theoretical and Empirical Investigations*, University of Chicago Press.

Mills, D., Branford, A., Inouye, K., Robinson, N. and Kingori, P. (2021) 'Fake' Journals and the Fragility of Authenticity: Citation Indexes, 'Predatory' Publishing and the African Research Ecosystem, *Journal of African Cultural Studies*, **33** (3), 276–96, https://doi.org/10.1080/13696815.2020.1864304.

Moher, D., Bouter, L., Kleinert, S., Glasziou, P., Sham, M. H., Barbour, V., Coriat, A. M., Foeger, N. and Dirnagl, U. (2020) The Hong Kong Principles for Assessing Researchers: Fostering Research Integrity, *PLoS Biology*, **18** (7), https://doi.org/10.1371/journal.pbio.3000737.

Morais, R., Stoy, L. and Borrell-Damián, L. (2019) 2019 Big Deals Report: An Updated Mapping of Major Scholarly Publishing Contracts in Europe,

European University Association, https://eua.eu/resources/publications/829:2019-big-deals-survey-report.html.

Muhonen, R., Benneworth, P. and Olmos-Peñuela, J. (2020) From Productive Interactions to Impact Pathways: Understanding the Key Dimensions in Developing SSH Research Societal Impact, *Research Evaluation*, **29** (1), 34–47, https://doi.org/10.1093/reseval/rvz003.

NABI (National Alliance for Broader Impacts) (2018) *The Current State of Broader Impacts: Advancing Science and Benefiting Society*, https://broaderimpacts.net/wp-content/uploads/2018/01/nabi-current-state-of-bi-011118.pdf.

Nabyonga-Orem, J., Asamani, J. A., Nyirenda, T. and Abimbola, S. (2020) Article Processing Charges are Stalling the Progress of African Researchers: A Call for Urgent Reforms, *BMJ Global Health* **5** (9), article 9, https://doi.org/10.1136/bmjgh-2020-003650.

National Academies of Sciences, Engineering and Medicine (2019) *Reproducibility and Replicability in Science*, National Academies Press, https://doi.org/10.17226/25303.

Nature (n.d.) www.nature.com/nature/for-authors/editorial-criteria-and-processes.

Nature Editorial (2023) Tools Such as ChatGPT Threaten Transparent Science: Here are our Ground Rules for Their Use, *Nature*, **613**, 612, https://doi.org/10.1038/d41586-023-00191-1.

Neylon, C., Ozaygen, A., Montgomery, L., Huang, H-K., Pyne, R., Lucraft, M. and Emery, C. (2021) More Readers in More Places: The Benefits of Open Access for Scholarly Books, *Insights*, **34** (1), http://doi.org/10.1629/uksg.558.

NISO (n.d.) CRediT: Contributor Roles Taxonomy, https://credit.niso.org.

Nogrady, B. (2023) Hyperauthorship: The Publishing Challenges for 'Big Team' Science, www.nature.com/articles/d41586-023-00575-3.

Okerson, A. and Holzman, A. (2015) *The Once and Future Publishing Library*, Council on Library and Information Resources, www.clir.org/pubs/reports/pub166.

OpenAPC (n.d.) https://treemaps.openapc.net/apcdata/openapc.

Oransky, I. (2022a) Publisher Retracts 350 Papers at Once, *Retraction Watch*, https://retractionwatch.com/2022/02/23/publisher-retracts-350-papers-at-once.

Oransky, I. (2022b) Physics Publisher Retracting Nearly 500 Likely Paper Mill Papers, *Retraction Watch*, https://retractionwatch.com/2022/09/09/physics-publisher-retracting-nearly-500-likely-paper-mill-papers.

O'Sullivan, Ma, L. and Doran, P. (2021) An Overview of Post-Publication Peer Review, *Scholarly Assessment Reports*, **3** (1), 6, http://doi.org/10.29024/sar.26.

Penfield, T., Baker, M. J., Scoble, R. and Wykes, M. C. (2014) Assessment, Evaluations and Definitions of Research Impact: A Review, *Research Evaluation*, **23** (1), 21–32, https://doi.org/10.1093/reseval/rvt021.

Perron, B. E., Hiltz-Perron, O. T. and Victor, B. G. (2019) Revealed: The Inner Workings of a Paper Mill, *Retraction Watch*, https://retractionwatch.com/2021/12/20/revealed-the-inner-workings-of-a-paper-mill.

Petrescu, M. and Krishen, A. (2022) The Evolving Crisis of the Peer Review Process, *Journal of Marketing Analytics*, **10**, 185–6, https://doi.org/10.1057/s41270-022-00176-5.

Piller, C. and Servick, K. (2020) Two Elite Medical Journals Retract Coronavirus Papers Over Data Integrity Questions, https://doi.org/10.1126/science.abd1697.

PLOS (n.d.) Open Peer Review, https://plos.org/resource/open-peer-review.

Portwood-Stacer, L. (2021) *The Book Proposal Book: A Guide for Scholarly Authors*, Princeton University Press.

Publon (2018) Global State of Peer Review Report, https://publons.com/community/gspr.

Ross-Hellauer, T. (2017) What is Open Peer Review? A Systematic Review, *F1000 Research*, **6** (588), https://doi.org/10.12688/f1000research.11369.2.

Ross-Hellauer, T. and Görögh, E. (2019) Guidelines for Open Peer Review Implementation, *Research Integrity and Peer Review*, **4** (4), https://doi.org/10.1186/s41073-019-0063-9.

Royster, P. (2014) Library Publishing is Special: Selection and Eligibility in Library Publishing, *Journal of Librarianship and Scholarly Communication*, **2** (4), eP1183, http://dx.doi.org/10.7710/2162-3309.1183.

Rumsey, S. (2021) Licence to Publish: The Boot is on the Wrong Foot, www.coalition-s.org/blog/licence-to-publish.

Scholarly Kitchen (n.d.) https://scholarlykitchen.sspnet.org.

Scopus (n.d.-a) www.elsevier.com/solutions/scopus/how-scopus-works/metrics/citescore.

Scopus (n.d.-b) Content Policy and Selection, www.elsevier.com/solutions/scopus/how-scopus-works/content/content-policy-and-selection.

Shearer, K., Chan, L., Kuchma, I. and Mounier, P. (2020) Fostering Bibliodiversity in Scholarly Communications: A Call for Action, *Zenodo*, https://doi.org/10.5281/zenodo.3752923.

Shen, H. (2020) Meet This Super-Spotter of Duplicated Images in Science Papers, *Nature*, **581**, 132–6, https://doi.org/10.1038/d41586-020-01363-z.

Sivertsen, G. and Meijer, I. (2020) Normal Versus Extraordinary Societal Impact: How to Understand, Evaluate and Improve Research Activities in their Relations to Society?, *Research Evaluation*, **29** (1), 66–70, https://doi.org/10.1093/reseval/rvz032.

Stoneman, S. and Hiremath, S. (2020) Twitter-Based Journal Clubs: Bringing Critical Appraisal to the Social Table, *Seminars in Nephrology*, **40** (3), 264–72, https://doi.org/10.1016/j.semnephrol.2020.04.004.

Stoy, L., Morais, R. and Borrell-Damián, L. (2019) Decrypting the Big Deal Landscape: Follow-Up of the 2019 EUA Big Deals Survey Report, European University Association, https://eua.eu/resources/publications/889:decrypting-the-big-deal-landscape.html.

Suber, P. (2012) *Open Access*, MIT Press.

Sugimoto, C. (2019) New Open-Access Journal Quantitative Science Studies, www.issi-society.org/blog/posts/2019/january/the-international-society-for-scientometrics-and-informetrics-ends-support-for-journal-of-informetrics-launches-new-open-access-journal-quantitative-science-studies.

UKRI (n.d.) https://impact.ref.ac.uk/casestudies.

UKRI (2022) REF Impact, www.ukri.org/about-us/research-england/research-excellence/ref-impact.

UKSG Insights (n.d.) https://insights.uksg.org/about/editorialpolicies.

UNESCO (2021) UNESCO Recommendation on Open Science, https://unesdoc.unesco.org/ark:/48223/pf0000379949.

University of Manchester (n.d.) https://documents.manchester.ac.uk/display.aspx?DocID=46134.

University of Toronto Press (2022) www.utpjournals.press/about/open-access.

Unsworth, J. M. (2014) Pubrarians and Liblishers at 20: reflections on library publishing from 1995–2014, *Journal of Librarianship and Scholarly Communication*, **2** (4), eP1201, http://dx.doi.org/10.7710/2162-3309.1201.

US Copyright Office (n.d.) www.copyright.gov/what-is-copyright.

Verbeke, D. and Mesotten, L. (2022) Library Funding for Open Access at KU Leuven, *Insights*, **35** (1), http://doi.org/10.1629/uksg.565.

Vollmer, T. (2022) Creative Commons and Open Access in an Academic Library: Implementation, Tools, Policy and Education. In Croates, J., Owen, V. and Reilly, S (eds), *Navigating Copyright for Libraries*, 378–404, De Gruyter Saur.

Waltman, L. and van Eck, N. J. (2012) The Inconsistency of the H-Index, *Journal of the American Society for Information Science and Technology*, **63** (2), 406–15, https://doi.org/10.1002/asi.21678.

Watermeyer, R. (2016) Impact in the REF: Issues and Obstacles, *Studies in Higher Education*, **41** (2), 199–214, https://doi.org/10.1080/03075079.2014.915303.

Weinberg, J. (2023) https://dailynous.com/2023/04/27/wiley-removes-goodin-as-editor-of-the-journal-of-political-philosophy.

Wellcome Trust (2020) What Researchers Think About the Culture They Work in, https://wellcome.org/reports/what-researchers-think-about-research-culture.

White House (2022) OSTP Issues Guidance to Make Federally Funded Research Freely Available Without Delay, www.whitehouse.gov/ostp/news-updates/2022/08/25/ostp-issues-guidance-to-make-federally-funded-research-freely-available-without-delay.

Wiley Author Services (n.d.) https://authorservices.wiley.com/author-resources/Journal-Authors/licensing/index.html.

Wiley Publishing (2022) https://authorservices.wiley.com/open-research/open-access/index.html.

Willinsky, J. (2022) *Copyright's Broken Promise: how to restore the law's ability to promote the progress of science*, MIT Press.

Wilsdon, J., Allen, L., Belfiore, E., Campbell, P., Curry, S., Hill, S., Jones, R., Kain, R., Kerridge, S., Thelwall, M., Tinkler, J., Viney, I., Wouters, P., Hill, J. and Johnson, B. (2015) *The Metric Tide: Report of the Independent Review of the Role of Metrics in Research Assessment and Management*, Sage, https://doi.org/10.13140/RG.2.1.4929.1363.

Wolfram, D., Wang, P., Hembree, A. and Park, H. (2020) Open Peer Review: Promoting Transparency in Open Science, *Scientometrics*, **125** (2), 1033–51, https://doi.org/10.1007/s11192-020-03488-4.

Wood, D. M. (2015) Spies in the Information Economy: Academic Publishers and the Trade in Personal Information, *ACME: An International Journal for Critical Geographies*, **8** (3), 484–93, www.acme-journal.org/index.php/acme/article/view/846.

Index

African Journals Online (AJOL) 37
Altmetric 69, 81
AmeliCA 37
article-processing charge (APC) 17, 32, 104, 105
author accepted manuscript (AAM) 22, 29, 44, 47
author guidelines 18
authorship 92–6
  authorship policy 93–4
  ghost authorship 93
  gift authorship 93–4

Berlin Declaration on Open Access to Knowledge in the Sciences and Humanities 28
Bethesda Statement on Open Access Publishing 28
bibliodiversity 33, 35, 72, 109–11, 112
'Big Deals' publishers 3, 104, 105, 107
blogs 23–4, 81
book chapters 13
book processing charge (BPC) 14, 33
book proposal 12, 55
Budapest Open Access Initiative (BOAI) 27

CiteScore 16, 65, 71

CoARA (Coalition for Advancing Research Assessment) 75
Committee on Publication Ethics (COPE) 97, 101
communism 91
conference proceedings 20
copyright transfer 21, 42, 44
Creative Commons (CC) licences 32, 44, 45–7
CRediT (Contributor Roles Taxonomy) 4, 95–6
crossover books 11

desk reject 54
digital object identifier (DOI) 70
Directory of Open Access Journals (DOAJ) 17, 32
disinterestedness 91
DORA (San Francisco Declaration of Research Assessment) 73

edited books 13
embargo period 23, 29
epistemic injustice 72
ESAC Transformative Agreement Registry 32
exclusive licence to publish 21

fabrication and falsification 98
field-weighted citation impact (FWCI) 68

fraudulent research 56, 92, 100
funding mandates 6, 8, 34

Garfield, Eugene 63, 71
generative AI 100–1, 113
Goodhart's Law 72
Google Scholar 70

Helsinki Initiative on Multilingualism in Scholarly Communication 110
h-index 69
Hong Kong Manifesto 73–4
hyperauthorship 4, 93

impact assessment
  attribution 86
  counterfactual argument 86
  ex ante 83–4
  ex post 83–4
impact case study 84
impact statement 83, 84
Institute for Scientific Information (ISI) 63, 71
institutional repositories 30
intellectual property 41, 107

journal articles 14
journal impact factor (JIF) 16, 63, 64–5, 109
journal policies 18

large language models 100
Leiden Manifesto 73
library publishing 14, 35, 36–7, 112
licence to publish 43–5, 47
logic model 77

Matthew effect 72
Mertonian norms 91
Metric Tide Report 74–5

monographs 11
multilingualism 109–11, 112

new university presses (NUP) 33, 37

oligopolistic publishers 104–6, 112
open access
  diamond 30–1, 76, 107
  gold 32–3, 109, 111, 112
  green 28–30, 107
Open Library of Humanities 34
open monographs 14, 33–4
open peer review 58–60
open research 107–9
open research infrastructure 3
Open Textbook Initiative 37, 112
ORCID 70
organised sceptism 91

paper mills 56, 57, 93, 96–7, 100, 108
peer review
  biases 56, 110
  conferences 55
  confirmation bias 58
  conservatism 58
  double-blind peer review 56–7
  fake peer review 97
  journal articles 14, 54
  monographs 12, 55
  peer-review rings 97
  single-blind peer review 57
peer review crisis 57, 58
plagiarism 56, 94–5
Plan S 34
platformisation 105–6, 108
podcasts 24–5, 80, 82
post-publication peer review 60
predatory journals 19–20, 32, 70, 110

preprints 18, 22–3
print on demand 33
privacy 106, 113
public engagement 24, 25, 78, 81, 89
publish or perish 3, 5, 63, 101
PubPeer 98

reproducibility 97–8, 99, 107
research for policy 82–3
research metrics
   article-level 67–9
   composite 69–70
   journal-level 64–7
responsible metrics 72, 108–9
retraction 92, 99–100
Retraction Watch 97
rights retention 47

scholar-led publications 2, 108
SciELO 37, 110
Science Citation Index (SCI) 63, 64

SCImago Journal Rank (SJR) 16, 65–6, 71
Scopus 16, 31, 32, 71, 76, 109
self-archiving 28, 30, 44
self-plagiarism 21, 95
serials crisis 28
social media 87
source normalised impact per paper (SNIP) 66, 71
subscribe to open (S2O) 14, 33

transformative agreements 32

UK REF 77, 84, 85
universalism 91
university rankings 3

version of record (VoR) 22–3, 31
vertical integration 3, 4, 106
videocasts 25

Web of Science (WoS) 16, 31, 32, 64, 71, 76, 97, 109